100 MENTAL MATHS

100 MENTAL MATHS ACTIVITIES

YEAR 2

Caroline Clissold and
Margaret Gronow

Authors
Caroline Clissold
Margaret Gronow

Illustrations
Debbie Clark

Series Designer
Sonja Bagley

Designer
Quadrum Solutions Ltd.

Mixed Sources
Product group from well-managed
forests and other controlled sources
www.fsc.org Cert no. TT-COC-002769
© 1996 Forest Stewardship Council
FSC

Text © Caroline Clissold
and Margaret Gronow
© 2010 Scholastic Ltd

Designed using Adobe InDesign

Published by Scholastic Ltd
Book End
Range Road,
Witney
Oxfordshire OX29 0YD

www.scholastic.co.uk

Printed by Bell and Bain Ltd, Glasgow

1 2 3 4 5 6 7 8 9   9 0 1 2 3 4 5 6 7 8

British Library Cataloguing-in-Publication Data
A catalogue record for this book is available from the British Library.

ISBN 978-1407-11416-3

The rights of Caroline Clissold and Margaret Gronow to be identified as the authors of this work have been asserted by them in accordance with the Copyright, Designs and Patents Act 1988.

Extracts from the Primary National Strategy's *Primary Framework for Mathematics* (2006) www.standards.dfes.gov.uk/primaryframework © Crown copyright. Reproduced under the terms of the Click Use Licence.

Coin images © Crown copyright, The Royal Mint.

CONTENTS

Introduction

About the series

100 Mental Maths Activities is a series of six photocopiable teachers' resource books, one for each of Years 1–6. Each book offers a bank of mental maths activities, each designed to last between five and ten minutes. The activities are designed to fit the planning guidelines of the *Renewed Framework for Teaching Mathematics* (2007) and are therefore divided into five Blocks with three Units of work in each Block.

This series provides a valuable accompaniment to *100 Maths Framework Lessons* (Scholastic, 2007). The mental maths activities are designed to accompany lessons in the framework series and grids are provided at the start of each Block to indicate the lesson and page numbers of the associated lesson plans in the relevant *100 Maths Framework Lessons* book. Used together, the teacher will have a rich bank of resources, activities and questions, offering greater choice and variety, while keeping to a closely similar mathematical content and progression. It is for the teacher to decide when to repeat an activity and when to move on: the exact mix of consolidation and progression needed will vary from one class to another. However, the series is also wholly appropriate for independent use alongside any maths scheme of work.

The six Rs of oral and mental work

In addition to matching the content of the Renewed Framework, this series also reflects the six features of children's mathematical learning that oral and mental work can support identified by the Primary National Strategy when renewing the Framework. The 'six Rs' provide a valuable guide to the purposes of each starter and a 'type of starter' is offered alongside each of the activities in this book.

The six types of starter include:

- rehearse: practicing and consolidating known skills

- recall: securing knowledge of facts - usually number facts

- refresh: drawing on, revisiting or assessing previous knowledge and skills

- refine: sharpening methods and procedures (eg mental strategies)

- read: using mathematical vocabulary and interpreting mathematical images, diagrams and vocabulary correctly

- reason: using and applying acquired knowledge and skills; using reasoning to draw conclusions.

For further information on the 'six Rs' visit the National Strategies website: *www.nationalstrategies.standards.dcsf.gov.uk*.

About the book

Each book provides support for teachers through 15 units of mental maths, developing and practising skills that will have been introduced, explained and explored in your main maths lesson time. Few resources are needed, and the questions for each activity are provided in full. The books are complete with answers, ready for you to pick up and use.

The activities are suitable for use with single- or mixed-ability groups and single- or mixed-age classes, as much emphasis has been placed on the use of differentiated and open-ended questions. Differentiated questions ensure that all the children can be included in each lesson and have the chance to succeed; suitable questions can be directed at chosen individuals, almost guaranteeing success and thus increased confidence.

Several essential photocopiable resource pages are also included (see pages 85–95). These resources are listed alongside each activity where required and should be prepared in advance of each mental maths session.

Each activity in this book has one or more learning objective based on the Year 2 teaching programme in the Renewed Framework. Curriculum grids are presented at the start of each Block to assist teachers with their planning and to highlight links with the related *100 Maths Framework Lessons* title. Alongside the activity description, required resources are highlighted, as well as the 'type of starter' (see above for further information). Where appropriate a 'mental strategy' for solving a number sentence or problem is suggested. Discussion of the children's methods is encouraged, since this will help the children to develop mathematical language skills: to appreciate that no single method is necessarily 'correct' and that a flexible repertoire of approaches is useful; to improve their overall confidence as they come to realise that all responses have value. Strategies are encouraged that will enable the children to progress from the known to the unknown number facts, thus developing their ability to select and use methods of mental calculation.

In Year 2, emphasis is placed on strategies for addition and subtraction (especially with numbers up to 30): adding from the larger number; partitioning; using doubles and 'near' doubles; counting up for a small difference. Repeated opportunities for counting in ones, twos, fives and tens will help to develop the children's understanding of patterns in times tables. Some lessons are based on telling the time and on using money. Games are included in each term's work to help provide variety and generate enthusiasm for numbers. Open-ended questions are used to challenge the children and extend their thinking.

The completion of the work in this book gives a sound basis for work in Year 3 and subsequent years, covered by the later books in the series. By following the lessons in this series of books, children will develop a variety of strategies for the solution of mathematical problems and will learn to be flexible in their approach to numerical work.

Transitional assessments

Transition is a time when, historically, children dip in their performance. Why this occurs is open to discussion but schools are increasingly aware of the need to accurately track children during these periods in order to ensure, as far as possible, a smooth learning journey. Transitional assessment is therefore important not just as a tool for summative judgements at the end of a school year, but also for communicating with teaching colleagues across the school.

100 Mental Maths Activities Year 2 includes two photocopiable single-level transitional assessments – both an oral and practical assessment and an oral and mental test – for levels 1 and 2, which will provide evidence of where children have reached in relation to national standards. Printable tests, mark schemes and answer sheets are available on pages 96-111.

BLOCK A

Unit 1

100 Mental Maths Starters				100 Maths Lessons		
Page	Objective	Activity title	Starter type	Unit	Lesson	Page
8	Read and write two-digit and three-digit numbers in figures and words.	**1** Read number words to 20	Read	1	4	12
8	Read and write two-digit and three-digit numbers in figures and words; describe and extend number sequences and recognise odd and even numbers.	**2** Write it!	Read	1	6	13, 14
9	Explain what each digit in a two-digit number represents, including numbers where 0 is a place holder; partition two-digit numbers in different ways, including into multiples of 10 and 1.	**3** How many tens and ones?	Refresh	1	5	13
9	Order two-digit numbers and position them on a number line; use the 'greater than' (>) and 'less than' (<) symbols.	**4** Order, order	Rehearse	1	7	15
10	Add or subtract mentally a one-digit number or a multiple of 10 to or from any two-digit number.	**5** 10 more, 10 less	Recall	1	8	15, 16
11	Understand that subtraction is the inverse of addition and vice versa; use this to derive and record related addition and subtraction number sentences.	**6** Inversions	Reason	1	9	16

Unit 2

100 Mental Maths Starters				100 Maths Lessons		
Page	Objective	Activity title	Starter type	Unit	Lesson	Page
12	Describe and extend number sequences and recognise odd and even numbers.	**7** Recognising odds and evens	Recall	2	1	21, 22
13	Read and write two-digit and three-digit numbers in figures and words; describe and extend number sequences and recognise odd and even numbers.	**8** Number sequences	Read	2	2	22
13	Count up to 100 objects by grouping them and counting in tens, fives or twos.	**9** Counting in fives	Recall	2	4	23, 24
14	Add or subtract mentally a one-digit number or a multiple of 10 to or from any two-digit number.	**10** 10 more or less	Recall	2	7	26

Unit 2 ...continued

	100 Mental Maths Starters			100 Maths Lessons		
Page	Objective	Activity title	Starter type	Unit	Lesson	Page
15	Add or subtract mentally a one-digit number or a multiple of 10 to or from any two-digit number.	⑪ 10 more	Recall	2	8	26, 27
16	Add or subtract mentally a one-digit number or a multiple of 10 to or from any two-digit number; use practical and informal written methods to add and subtract two-digit numbers.	⑫ Adding two-digit numbers by partitioning	Refine	2	9	27

Unit 3

	100 Mental Maths Starters			100 Maths Lessons		
Page	Objective	Activity title	Starter type	Unit	Lesson	Page
17	Explain what each digit in a two-digit number represents, including numbers where 0 is a place holder; partition two-digit numbers in different ways, including into multiples of 10 and 1.	⑬ What's my value?	Reason	3	6	37, 38
17	Order two-digit numbers and position them on a number line; use the 'greater than' (>) and 'less than' (<) symbols.	⑭ Greater, less than, in between?	Recall	3	2	34, 35
18	Round two-digit numbers to the nearest 10.	⑮ Nearest 10	Recall	3	3	35
19	Use practical and informal written methods to add and subtract two-digit numbers.	⑯ Add 9, subtract 9	Refine	3	5	36
20	Use practical and informal written methods to add and subtract two-digit numbers.	⑰ Partitioning to add	Refine	3	9	39
21	Use practical and informal written methods to add and subtract two-digit numbers.	⑱ Adding: larger number first and partition	Refine	3	10	39

BLOCK A

(1) **Read number words to 20**

Resources A set of number word cards (from photocopiable page 87); a board or flipchart	**Learning objective** Read and write two-digit and three-digit numbers in figures and words. **Type of starter** Read
No set answers	Sit the children facing the board or flipchart. Hold up a card showing a number word. The children must say the number aloud together. Choose a child to write the matching numeral on the board each time. Continue until all of the cards have been used. 

(2) **Write it!**

Resources Whiteboards and pens; numeral cards from 0–9 (from photocopiable page 85); a board or flipchart	**Learning objective** Read and write two-digit and three-digit numbers in figures and words; describe and extend number sequences and recognise odd and even numbers. **Type of starter** Read
No set answers	Using the set of numeral cards, invite three children to pick one each. Stick or write them on the board. Ask the children to write all the two-digit numbers they can find from the cards. For example, from 2, 6 and 9: 26, 29, 62, 69, 92, 96. Ask them to read each one to a partner. Take feedback from the class, writing the numbers they say on the board. Ask them to write the numbers in order from smallest to greatest on their whiteboards and then to circle the even numbers and underline the odd numbers. Recap the place value of each number. If you wish, ask the children to write the numbers as words.

(3) How many tens and ones?

Learning objective
Explain what each digit in a two-digit number represents, including numbers where 0 is a place holder; partition two-digit numbers in different ways, including into multiples of 10 and 1.

Type of starter
Refresh

Mental strategies
When asked, they should say the answer and then say how many tens and ones it is (for example: touch 27, add 10, say '37, 3 tens and 7 ones').

Resources
A 0–99 square (from photocopiable page 89) for each child

Ask the children to touch the number that you say, and then to add 10 to it.

1. 25
2. 32
3. 59
4. 14
5. 61
6. 48
7. 76
8. 50
9. 83
10. 37

Answers
1. 3 tens 5 ones
2. 4 tens 2 ones
3. 6 tens 9 ones
4. 2 tens 4 ones
5. 7 tens 1 one
6. 5 tens 8 ones
7. 8 tens 6 ones
8. 6 tens 0 ones
9. 9 tens 3 ones
10. 4 tens 7 ones

(4) Order, order

Learning objective
Order two-digit numbers and position them on a number line; use the 'greater than' (>) and 'less than' (<) symbols.

Type of starter
Rehearse

Resources
Whiteboards and pens; numeral cards to 100; a board or flipchart

Invite five children to pick a numeral card from a pile you have in front of you. Ask the class to order the children from the one holding the lowest number to the one holding the highest.

Ask everyone to draw a number line on their whiteboards and to plot the numbers where they think they should go.

Check with them by drawing an empty number line on the board. Discuss and plot some helpful marker numbers: 50, 25 and 75.

Write '<' on the board and ask the children to write two numbers either side of it. Repeat for '>'.

Repeat this whole procedure with different sets of five numbers.

No set answers

BLOCK A

⑤ 10 more, 10 less

Resources	Learning objective
None	Add or subtract mentally a one-digit number or a multiple of 10 to or from any two-digit number.
	Type of starter
	Recall

Answers

1. 30
2. 90
3. 50
4. 80
5. 20
6. 60
7. 100
8. 40

9. 30
10. 50
11. 70
12. 10
13. 60
14. 40
15. 20
16. 80

The children raise a hand to give you the number that is 10 more or less than the 'tens' number you will say. For example: *10 more than 30 is...* '40.'

What is 10 more than...?

1.	20	5.	10
2.	80	6.	50
3.	40	7.	90
4.	70	8.	30

What is 10 less than...?

9.	40	13.	70
10.	60	14.	50
11.	80	15.	30
12.	20	16.	90

⑥ Inversions

Learning objective	**Resources**
Understand that subtraction is the inverse of addition and vice versa; use this to derive and record related addition and subtraction number sentences.	Whiteboards and pens; a board or flipchart
Type of starter Reason	

Draw an inversion loop, such as this one, on the board.

No set answers

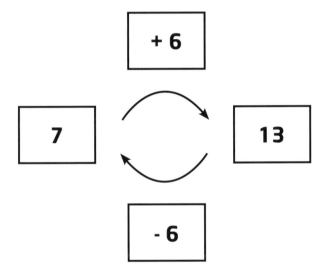

Ask the children what they think it means.

Next, write a different number on the left and ask the children to tell you what number must go on the right. Repeat this a few times with different numbers.

Now, write a number on the right and ask the children to work out what must go on the left. Repeat this a few times, always reinforcing the fact that addition and subtraction are inverse operations.

Ask them to make up some inversion loops of their own and to share them with a partner.

Write some missing number sentences on the board and ask the children to work out the missing number, for example: $12 + ? = 24$, $13 - ? = 8$, $? + 9 = 20$, $? - 10 = 5$. They could draw inversion loops if it will help them.

Discuss strategies used to work out the answers, for example: did they do the inverse operation? Did they count on/back?

BLOCK A

⑦ Recognising odds and evens

Resources	Learning objective
None	Describe and extend number sequences and recognise odd and even numbers.
	Type of starter
	Recall

Answers

1. even
2. odd
3. even
4. even
5. odd
6. odd

Sit the children in a circle and ask them to count in twos from 0 to 30 and back again.

Repeat, choosing a different child to begin the count. Ask: *Have we counted even or odd numbers?*

Remind the children that even numbers are all numbers in the 'twos' family, while odd numbers are not.

Repeat the activity, counting in twos from 1 to 31 and back again. Ask: *Have we counted even or odd numbers?*

Ask an individual to say whether the number is odd or even, and to explain how they know (if possible).

1. 8
2. 11
3. 4
4. 10
5. 15
6. 7

SCHOLASTIC

BLOCK A

 Number sequences

Learning objective	Resources
Read and write two-digit and three-digit numbers in figures and words; describe and extend number sequences and recognise odd and even numbers. **Type of starter** Read	Whiteboards and pens; a board or flipchart

Write this sequence of numbers on the board: 12, 14, 16, 18. Ask the children to write the next five numbers on their whiteboards and to tell you anything they notice about the sequence, for example: all even numbers, increases in steps of two, two-digit numbers.

Repeat with this sequence: 21, 19, 17, 15 (decreases in steps of two, all odd numbers, two-digit numbers).

Write up some more, varying them so that they increase and decrease in steps of three, four, five and ten.

Ask the children to make a sequence of their own and to write it on their whiteboard. They should then pass it to a partner to complete.

Take feedback, inviting a few of the children to write their sequences on the board for the class to continue. For each one, ask them to tell you about the sequence.

No set answers

 Counting in fives

Learning objective	Resources
Count up to 100 objects by grouping them and counting in tens, fives or twos. **Type of starter** Recall	None

Sit the children in a circle and count together in fives from 0 to 100 and back again. Then count around the circle in fives from 0 to 50 and back again.

Repeat, choosing a different child to start the count each time. Play the game at an increasingly fast pace.

No set answers

BLOCK A

⑩ **10 more or less**

Resources	Learning objective
None	Add or subtract mentally a one-digit number or a multiple of 10 to or from any two-digit number.

SCHOLASTIC

Type of starter
Recall

Mental strategy
Vary the pace to keep the activity lively.

Answers

1. 50
2. 80
3. 0
4. 50
5. 40
6. 40
7. 10
8. 70
9. 10
10. 100

Ask the children to listen very carefully. You will say a tens number and then say '10 more' or '10 less'. They should raise a hand to give the answer.

1.   40, 10 more

2.   70, 10 more

3.   10, 10 less

4.   60, 10 less

5.   30, 10 more

6.   50, 10 less

7.   0, 10 more

8.   80, 10 less

9.   20, 10 less

10. 90, 10 more

⑪ 10 more

Learning objective	Resources
Add or subtract mentally a one-digit number or a multiple of 10 to or from any two-digit number.	None
Type of starter	
Recall	
Mental strategy	
After the first three, ask the children for their strategies. Collect several and discuss.	

Ask the children to add the number you say on to 10.

1.	4	6.	8
2.	7	7.	3
3.	9	8.	1
4.	2	9.	5
5.	6		

Ask the children to add 10 to the number you say.

10.	13	15.	16
11.	18	16.	11
12.	15	17.	14
13.	19	18.	17
14.	12		

Answers

1. 14
2. 17
3. 19
4. 12
5. 16
6. 18
7. 13
8. 11
9. 15

10. 23
11. 28
12. 25
13. 29
14. 22
15. 26
16. 21
17. 24
18. 27

BLOCK A

(12) Adding two-digit numbers by partitioning

Resources A board or flipchart	**Learning objective** Add or subtract mentally a one-digit number or a multiple of 10 to or from any two-digit number; use practical and informal written methods to add and subtract two-digit numbers. **Type of starter** Refine

Answers

1. 25
2. 26
3. 27
4. 24
5. 25
6. 26
7. 28
8. 24
9. 29
10. 23

Write:

$$12 + 14 =$$

Ask: *How shall we find the answer?* Collect several suggestions.

Encourage partitioning:	10 + 2 + 10 + 4
Adding tens is easy!	10 + 10 = 20
Now add the ones:	2 + 4 = 6

Now recombine:

$$20 + 6 = 26$$

Write each example. Encourage the children to explain how they found the answer.

1. 13 + 12
2. 15 + 11
3. 14 + 13
4. 12 + 12
5. 11 + 14

6. 14 + 12
7. 15 + 13
8. 13 + 11
9. 15 + 14
10. 12 + 11

What's my value?

Learning objective Explain what each digit in a two-digit number represents, including numbers where 0 is a place holder; partition two-digit numbers in different ways, including into multiples of 10 and 1. **Type of starter** Reason	**Resources** Whiteboards and pens; a board or flipchart

Write '54' on the board. Ask the children what each digit is worth. Ask them to write some number sentences on their whiteboards to show how the number is made. Take feedback and write the number sentences they suggest on the board. Aim for: 50 + 4 = 54, 40 + 14 = 54, 30 + 24 = 54, 20 + 34 = 54, 10 + 44 = 54. Repeat for other numbers, such as 27, 68 and 33. Write a two-digit multiple of 10 on the board and ask the children what the zero represents (it is the place holder for the units/ones number). Ask the children to write down what the number would be without the place holder. Repeat with a few more of these numbers. Repeat this for a few three-digit numbers, for example: 104. Each time, ask what the number would be without the place holder, for example: 14.	**No set answers**

 Greater, less than, in between?

Learning objective Order two-digit numbers and position them on a number line; use the 'greater than' (>) and 'less than' (<) symbols. **Type of starter** Recall **Mental strategy** Ask the children to listen carefully to each question or instruction and raise a hand to answer.	**Resources** None

1. Which number is greater, 30 or 70?
2. Which is the smaller number, 25 or 55?
3. Give me a number more than 30.
4. Give me a number less than 16.
5. Give me a number between 70 and 80.
6. Give me a number between 41 and 51.
7. Which is the larger number, 27 or 72?
8. Which is the smaller number, 39 or 34?
9. Give me a number between 19 and 11.
10. Which number is greater, 52 or 32?

Answers

1. 70
2. 25
3. Anything > 30
4. Anything < 16
5. Anything >70 < 80
6. Anything >41 < 51
7. 72
8. 34
9. Anything >11 <19
10. 52

BLOCK A

(15) Nearest 10

Resources	**Learning objective**
A 0-99 square (enlarged from photocopiable page 89)	Round two-digit numbers to the nearest 10.
	Type of starter
	Recall
	Mental strategy
	Remind the children of the rule that numbers ending in 5 round up.

Answers

1. 20
2. 50
3. 60
4. 40
5. 80
6. 10
7. 10
8. 50
9. 100
10. 0
11. 80
12. 60
13. 20
14. 80
15. 40
16. 80

Sit the children facing the 0-99 square.

Point to a number and say it, then ask a child to round the number to the nearest 10.

1.	23	9.	96
2.	49	10.	3
3.	61	11.	77
4.	37	12.	55
5.	84	13.	19
6.	12	14.	82
7.	8	15.	38
8.	45	16.	76

Add 9, subtract 9

Learning objective	Resources
Use practical and informal written methods to add and subtract two-digit numbers.	None

Type of starter
Refine

Mental strategies
Play at a fast pace to encourage rapid recall.

In the second part, encourage the strategy 'take away 10 then add 1'.

Discuss the usual strategy for adding 9: 'add 10 and take away 1'.

Ask individual children to add 9 to a number. For example, say:
My number is 14, Katy, so your number is…'23'?

1.	16	6.	21
2.	19	7.	17
3.	12	8.	25
4.	15	9.	18
5.	28	10.	13

Ask: *Who can remember a quick way to subtract 9?*

Ask the children to subtract 9 from these numbers:

11.	25	16.	36
12.	27	17.	33
13.	22	18.	29
14.	14	19.	26
15.	24	20.	23

Answers

1. 25
2. 28
3. 21
4. 24
5. 37
6. 30
7. 26
8. 34
9. 27
10. 22

11. 16
12. 18
13. 13
14. 5
15. 15
16. 27
17. 24
18. 20
19. 17
20. 14

(17) Partitioning to add

Resources	Learning objective
A board or flipchart	Use practical and informal written methods to add and subtract two-digit numbers.

Type of starter
Refine

Mental strategies
Write each example.

Encourage children to explain how they found the answers.

Answers

1. 26
2. 27
3. 23
4. 28
5. 28
6. 25
7. 29
8. 26
9. 25
10. 27

Write:

$$13 + 15 =$$

Ask: *How shall we find the answer?*

Collect several suggestions.

Encourage partitioning:	10 + 3 + 10 + 5
Adding tens is easy!	10 + 10 = 20
Now add the ones:	3 + 5 = 8

Now recombine:

$$20 + 8 = 28$$

Write each example. Encourage the children to explain how they found the answer.

1.	11 + 15		6.	14 + 11
2.	14 + 13		7.	15 + 14
3.	12 + 11		8.	13 + 13
4.	14 + 14		9.	12 + 13
5.	13 + 15		10.	15 + 12

Adding: larger number first and partition

<table>
<tr><td colspan="2">

Learning objective
Use practical and informal written methods to add and subtract two-digit numbers.

Type of starter
Refine

Mental strategy
Encourage the children to explain the method used.

</td><td>

Resources
A board or flipchart

</td></tr>
</table>

Write:

$$12 + 25 =$$

Remind the children that it is often easier to add numbers by putting the larger number first.

Ask: *Which is larger, 12 or 25?*

Write: 25 + 12 =

Encourage counting on the tens, then adding on.

Write:

$$25 + 12 = 35 + 2 = 37$$

Write each example on the board and repeat the above procedure.

1.   12 + 16   6.   12 + 26

2.   11 + 18   7.   13 + 23

3.   16 + 22   8.   37 + 11

4.   25 + 14   9.   19 + 18

5.   22 + 18   10. 25 + 17

Answers
1.   28
2.   29
3.   38
4.   39
5.   40
6.   38
7.   36
8.   48
9.   37
10. 42

BLOCK B

Unit 1

	100 Mental Maths Starters			100 Maths Lessons		
Page	Objective	Activity title	Starter type	Unit	Lesson	Page
24	Solve problems involving addition, subtraction, multiplication or division in contexts of numbers, measures or pounds and pence.	(19) Naming and adding coins	Recall	1	7	50
24	Solve problems involving addition, subtraction, multiplication or division in contexts of numbers, measures or pounds and pence.	(20) Addition of two coins	Rehearse	1	8	50, 51
25	Derive and recall all addition and subtraction facts for each number to at least 10.	(21) Addition facts about 10	Recall	1	3	47, 48
26	Derive and recall all addition and subtraction facts for all pairs with totals to 20.	(22) Equals 20	Recall	1	6	49, 50
26	Derive and recall doubles of all numbers to 20.	(23) Quick doubles	Recall	1	9	51, 52
27	Derive and recall multiplication facts for the two-times table.	(24) Two-times table	Recall	1	10	52
28	Visualise common 3D solids; sort, make and describe shapes, referring to their properties.	(25) Which shape?	Rehearse	1	13	54
28	Visualise common 2D shapes; identify shapes from pictures of them in different positions and orientations; sort, make and describe shapes, referring to their properties.	(26) 2D shapes	Rehearse	1	15	55

Unit 2

	100 Mental Maths Starters			100 Maths Lessons		
Page	Objective	Activity title	Starter type	Unit	Lesson	Page
29	Solve problems involving addition in contexts of numbers, measures or pounds and pence.	(27) Addition of three coins	Rehearse	2	3	65, 66
29	Derive and recall all pairs with totals to 20.	(28) Pairs for 20	Rehearse	2	11	71
30	Derive and recall all addition and subtraction facts for each number to at least 20.	(29) How to make 20	Recall	2	13	72
30	Derive and recall multiplication facts for the two-times table.	(30) Two-times table facts	Recall	2	9	69
31	Derive and recall multiplication facts for the ten-times table.	(31) Ten-times table	Recall	2	10	70
31	Derive and recall multiplication facts for the five-times table.	(32) Five-times table	Refine	2	15	73

Unit 2 ...continued

	100 Mental Maths Starters			100 Maths Lessons		
Page	Objective	Activity title	Starter type	Unit	Lesson	Page
32	Visualise common 3D solids; sort, make and describe shapes, referring to their properties.	(33) What am I?	Reason	2	12	71, 72
32	Visualise common 2D shapes; identify shapes from pictures of them in different positions and orientations; sort, make and describe shapes, referring to their properties.	(34) Snap!	Reason	2	14	72, 73

Unit 3

	100 Mental Maths Starters			100 Maths Lessons		
Page	Objective	Activity title	Starter type	Unit	Lesson	Page
33	Solve problems involving addition, subtraction, multiplication or division in contexts of numbers, measures or pounds and pence.	(35) Spending and change	Rehearse	3	8	84, 85
34	Derive and recall all addition and subtraction facts for all pairs of multiples of 10 with totals up to 100.	(36) Make 10, make 100	Rehearse	3	1	80
35	Derive and recall all addition and subtraction facts for all pairs of multiples of 10 with totals up to 100.	(37) Make 100	Recall	3	2	80, 81
35	Derive and recall doubles of all numbers to 20.	(38) Building up doubling	Refine	3	3	81
36	Understand that halving is the inverse of doubling and derive and recall doubles of all numbers to 20, and the corresponding halves.	(39) Half is...	Recall	3	4	82
36	Understand that halving is the inverse of doubling and derive and recall doubles of all numbers to 20, and the corresponding halves.	(40) Double and halve	Recall	3	5	82
37	Visualise common 3D solids; identify shapes from pictures of them in different positions and orientations; sort, make and describe shapes, referring to their properties.	(41) Visualise	Rehearse	3	14	89
37	Visualise common 2D shapes; identify shapes from pictures of them in different positions and orientations; sort, make and describe shapes, referring to their properties.	(42) Draw me!	Rehearse	3	15	89

(19) Naming and adding coins

Resources
Sets of coin cards 20p, 10p, 5p, 2p, 1p (from photocopiable page 88), one card for each child

Learning objective
Solve problems involving addition, subtraction, multiplication or division in contexts of numbers, measures or pounds and pence.

Type of starter
Recall

Mental strategy
Encourage putting the larger coin first.

No set answers

Sit the children in a circle and give each child a card up to 20p.

Ask two children to stand, hold up their cards and name them. Ask the group how they would add these coins together. Ask a third child to say the total.

Repeat, making sure each child takes a turn.

(20) Addition of two coins

Resources
Sets of coin cards 50p, 20p, 10p, 5p, 2p and 1p (from photocopiable page 88), one card for each child

Learning objective
Solve problems involving addition, subtraction, multiplication or division in contexts of numbers, measures or pounds and pence.

Type of starter
Rehearse

No set answers

Sit the children in a circle. Hand out the coin cards, which include 50p.

Ask two children to stand in front of the group and show their cards. Choose a third child to say the total of the two coins.

Continue around the circle until each child has had a turn at standing with a card and at saying the total.

BLOCK B

(21) Addition facts about 10

Learning objective
Derive and recall all addition and subtraction facts for each number to at least 10.

Type of starter
Recall

Mental strategies
Explain that you will say a number (for example: 6), and they should hold up their card if their number adds to your number to make 10 (for example: 4).

Encourage rapid recall.

Resources
Enough shuffled sets of numeral cards 1–10 (from photocopiable page 85) for each child to have one card

Sit the children in a circle and give each child one numeral card.

Say: *Show me the number to add to… to make 10.*

1.	8	6.	2
2.	5	7.	4
3.	3	8.	0
4.	9	9.	1
5.	6	10.	7

The children can exchange cards and repeat the activity.

Answers
1. 2
2. 5
3. 7
4. 1
5. 4
6. 8
7. 6
8. 10
9. 9
10. 3

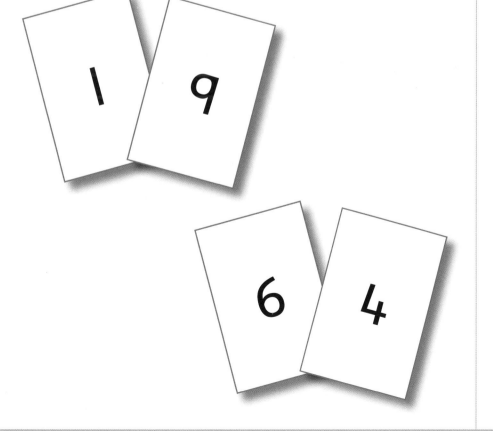

BLOCK B

(22) **Equals 20**

Resources
Shuffled sets of numeral cards 0–20 (from photocopiable pages 85 and 86), one card for each child

Learning objective
Derive and recall all addition and subtraction facts for all pairs with totals to 20.

Type of starter
Recall

Mental strategy
If the answer is incorrect, they can choose a neighbour to help them and have a second try.

No set answers

Stand the children in a circle and give each child a numeral card.

Play a game: the children take turns (around the circle) to make an addition sentence, using the number on their own card (for example: 12) and the number they need to make 20 (for example: 8).

They should say the sentence, for example: '12 add 8 equals 20'.

If they are correct, they sit down.

(23) **Quick doubles**

Resources
Numeral cards 1–10 (from photocopiable page 85), one card for each child

Learning objective
Derive and recall doubles of all numbers to 20.

Type of starter
Recall

No set answers

Sit the children in a circle to play a doubling game. Give each child a card.

Ask the children in turn round the circle to say the double of the number on their card, for example: 'double 3 is 6'.

Ask the children to respond quickly, one after another.

When each child has had a turn, collect the cards and give them out again to repeat the activity.

(24) Two-times table

Learning objective	Resources
Derive and recall multiplication facts for the two-times table.	A board or flipchart
Type of starter Recall	

Remind the children that 1 group of 2 equals 2, so 1 times 2 equals 2.

Write:

$$1 \times 2 = 2$$
$$2 \times 2 = 4$$
$$3 \times$$

Ask: *What shall I write next?* Continue building up the two-times table.

When the table is complete to 10 × 2, read each multiplication sentence aloud together ('1 times 2 equals 2...').

Ask individuals:

1. 4 times 2 equals...

2. 6 twos are...

3. 7 groups of 2 equal...

4. 5 groups of 2 equal...

5. 10 times 2 equals...

6. 8 groups of 2 equal...

7. 2 twos are...

8. 9 times 2 equals...

9. 1 two is...

10. 3 groups of 2 equal...

Answers

1. 8
2. 12
3. 14
4. 10
5. 20
6. 16
7. 4
8. 18
9. 2
10. 6

BLOCK B

(25) Which shape?

Resources Selection of 3D shapes: sphere, cube, cuboid, cone, cylinder, pyramid, one of each for a group of four children	**Learning objective** Visualise common 3D solids; sort, make and describe shapes, referring to their properties. **Type of starter** Rehearse

No set answers

Arrange the children into groups of four. Give each group a set of 3D shapes.

Give clues for each shape, in turn, that refer to: shape and number of faces, number of vertices and edges. For example:

- *My shape has at least one square face.* The children select the shapes that have at least one square face (cube, cuboid, pyramid).

- *It has six faces* (cube, cuboid).

- *Some of the faces are rectangular* (cuboid).

When the children have found the shape, they stand up. The first group standing wins a point.

Continue like this until all shapes have been described at least once.

The winning group is the one with the most points.

(26) 2D shapes

Resources Two sets of 2D shape cards (from photocopiable page 91)	**Learning objective** Visualise common 2D shapes; identify shapes from pictures of them in different positions and orientations; sort, make and describe shapes, referring to their properties. **Type of starter** Rehearse

No set answers

Give each child a shape card and ask them to identify the shape and tell a partner its properties of sides, corners and symmetry.

Ask the children to find another child that has a shape card with at least one property that is the same. Give them about a minute to do this.

Next, ask the pairs of children to find another pair with shapes that share a property.

Ask the children to stand up if their shape matches criteria you call out, for example: regular shape, hexagon, one or more lines of symmetry, eight sides, three corners.

(27) **Addition of three coins**

Learning objective Solve problems involving addition in contexts of numbers, measures or pounds and pence. **Type of starter** Rehearse **Mental strategy** Encourage putting the 'larger' coin first.	**Resources** Sets of coin cards 50p, 20p, 10p, 5p, 2p, 1p (from photocopiable page 88), one card for each child; three PE hoops

Sit the children in a semicircle and give each child a coin card. Place the three hoops (A, B and C) in a line at the front.

Ask the first three children each to stand in a hoop and show their cards to the group. Ask a fourth child to total the money on the cards.

If the answer is correct, the children in hoops A, B and C move along, so that the child in hoop C answers the next question and a new child moves to hoop A.

The game is continued until all the children in the semicircle have answered a question. If an incorrect answer is given, play passes to the next child.

No set answers

(28) **Pairs for 20**

Learning objective Derive and recall all pairs with totals to 20. **Type of starter** Rehearse	**Resources** Board or flipchart; set of numeral cards 0–20 (from photocopiable pages 85 and 86)

Draw two blank number lines: one from 1 to 10 and one from 10 to 20.

Remove the 0, 10 and 20 numeral cards before shuffling the set.

Ask a child to choose a card (for example: 8) and write the number above the appropriate line in the correct place. Continue until all numbers are in place.

Put back the 0, 10 and 20 cards and shuffle the cards again.

Ask a child to choose a card and write the number beneath the appropriate line in the correct place to make a pair totalling 20 (for example: 12 would go beneath 8). The child should say: '8 add 12 equals 20'.

The child who takes the 10 card should write 10 in the appropriate place on both number lines. Repeat this together. Continue until the lines are complete.

No set answers

BLOCK B

(29) How to make 20

Resources
Sets of numeral cards 0-10 (from photocopiable page 85), one card for each child; a set of numeral cards 11-20 (from photocopiable page 86)

Learning objective
Derive and recall all addition and subtraction facts for each number to at least 20.

Type of starter
Recall

No set answers

Give each child one of the numeral cards 0-10.

Hold up a card with a number from 11 to 20 (for example: 16). If the children have the number (for example: 4) that adds to your number to make 20, they should hold it up and say the number sentence: '16 add 4 makes 20'.

Repeat the number sentence together.

Repeat the activity until all the numeral cards 11-20 have been used twice.

(30) Two-times table facts

Resources
Even numeral cards 2-20 (from photocopiable pages 85 and 86), one card for each pair of children

Learning objective
Derive and recall multiplication facts for the two-times table.

Type of starter
Recall

Answers

1. 6
2. 10
3. 16
4. 2
5. 8
6. 14
7. 4
8. 20
9. 12
10. 18

Organise the class into mixed-ability pairs. Give each pair a numeral card.

If they have the answer to a question, they hold up the card and say the number.

Collect the cards and give them out again to repeat the activity.

1. 3 × 2
2. 5 × 2
3. 8 × 2
4. 1 × 2
5. 4 × 2
6. 7 × 2
7. 2 × 2
8. 10 × 2
9. 6 × 2
10. 9 × 2

(31) Ten-times table

Learning objective	**Resources**
Derive and recall multiplication facts for the ten-times table.	Ten numeral cards marked '10' (you could use the one on photocopiable page 85)
Type of starter	
Recall	

Count together in tens from 0 to 100 and back.

Give out the cards to ten children. Ask three children to stand up and show their cards. Ask: *How many tens is that altogether?*

All say: '3 tens make 30. 3 times 10 equals 30'.

1. 4 times 10
2. 2 times 10
3. 7 times 10
4. 5 times 10
5. 1 times 10

6. 9 times 10
7. 3 times 10
8. 10 times 10
9. 6 times 10
10. 8 times 10

Answers
1. 40
2. 20
3. 70
4. 50
5. 10
6. 90
7. 30
8. 100
9. 60
10. 80

(32) Five-times table

Learning objective	**Resources**
Derive and recall multiplication facts for the five-times table.	A board or flipchart
Type of starter	
Refine	

Draw a number line from 1 to 10. Write the multiples of 5 beneath the line (for example: 15 below 3) as the children recite the five-times table.

Children raise a hand to answer the questions.

1. 3×5
2. 6×5
3. 2×5
4. 9×5
5. 1×5

6. 5×5
7. 10×5
8. 7×5
9. 4×5
10. 8×5

Erase some of the better-known multiples and repeat the questions.

Answers
1. 15
2. 30
3. 10
4. 45
5. 5
6. 25
7. 50
8. 35
9. 20
10. 40

BLOCK B

(33) **What am I?**

Resources	**Learning objective**
Selection of 3D shapes: sphere, cube, cuboid, cone, cylinder, pyramid; bag	Visualise common 3D solids; sort, make and describe shapes, referring to their properties.
	Type of starter
	Reason

No set answers

Put the 3D shapes into a bag. Put your hand in the bag, feel one of the shapes and describe it to the children. They guess what it is from your description. Ensure you talk about the shape and the number of faces, edges and vertices. If they struggle to guess it, tell them where they would see the shape in real life.

Once they have guessed the shape, show it to them and together revise its properties and where they would see it in real life.

Invite children to play 'teacher' and describe a shape from the bag as you did.

Again, once guessed, revise properties and real-life examples.

(34) **Snap!**

Resources	**Learning objective**
2D shape cards (from photocopiable page 91) enlarged onto A3 paper; a board	Visualise common 2D shapes; identify shapes from pictures of them in different positions and orientations; sort, make and describe shapes, referring to their properties.
	Type of starter
	Reason

No set answers

Stick one of the shape cards on the board. Ask the children to describe it.

Turn the others over one at a time. Show each to the children. They look at the new shape and see if it matches the one on the board in any way. For example: has symmetry, is regular or irregular, has same number of sides, has same name. When there is a match, they call out 'snap'.

The first child to call 'snap' explains why and the others need to agree or disagree.

Stick the second shape on the board to make a pair, label them with their names and begin again.

Repeat until all the cards have been used.

(35) **Spending and change**

Learning objective
Solve problems involving addition, subtraction, multiplication or division in contexts of numbers, measures or pounds and pence.

Type of starter
Rehearse

Mental strategies
Encourage adding on.

Remind the children that 100p = £1.00.

Resources
None

Ask questions about spending money. Ask individuals to say how much change they will be given each time.

How much change do you get from 20p when you spend...?

1. 10p
2. 15p
3. 18p
4. 11p
5. 7p
6. 14p
7. 3p
8. 16p

How much change do you get from £1 when you spend...?

9. 90p
10. 50p
11. 70p
12. 20p
13. 80p
14. 60p
15. 30p
16. 10p

Answers
1. 10p
2. 5p
3. 2p
4. 9p
5. 13p
6. 6p
7. 17p
8. 4p
9. 10p
10. 50p
11. 30p
12. 80p
13. 20p
14. 40p
15. 70p
16. 90p

BLOCK B

36 **Make 10, make 100**

Resources A board or flipchart; a pointer	**Learning objective** Derive and recall all addition and subtraction facts for all pairs of multiples of 10 with totals up to 100. **Type of starter** Rehearse **Mental strategies** Play the game at an increasingly fast pace to encourage rapid recall. No one voice should be heard above the others.
No set answers	Draw a clock face as shown. When you point to a number, the children should say together the number that, when added to it, makes 10. Now add a zero to each number on the clock face. When you point to a number, the children should say the number that, when added to it, makes 100. Continue with the game.

(37) Make 100

| Learning objective
Derive and recall all addition and subtraction facts for all pairs of multiples of 10 with totals up to 100.

Type of starter
Recall

Mental strategy
Remind the children that they know the pairs making 10 (for example: 7 + 3), but their cards are showing 'tens' (for example: 7 tens and 3 tens). | **Resources**
Sets of numeral cards 10–100 (from photocopiable page 90), one card for each child |

Sit the children in a circle and give each child one of the shuffled cards.

Go around the circle. Ask each child to say the number on their card and what must be added to it to make 100 (for example: '70 and 30 make 100').

Collect the cards after each child has had a turn.

Shuffle and repeat the activity.

No set answers

(38) Building up doubling

| Learning objective
Derive and recall doubles of all numbers to 20.

Type of starter
Refine

Mental strategy
Encourage a quick pace. | **Resources**
Shuffled sets of numeral cards 1–10 (from photocopiable page 85), one card for each child |

Sit the children in a circle. Together, recite the two-times table.

Give each child one of the cards. Remind the children that 'double' a number is the same as 2 times the number, or the number added to itself.

For example:

$$\text{double } 3 = 2 \times 3 = 3 + 3 = 6$$

The children take turns around the circle saying double the number on their card, for example: 'double 3 equals 6'.

No set answers

(39) Half is...

Resources	Learning objective
None	Understand that halving is the inverse of doubling and derive and recall doubles of all numbers to 20, and the corresponding halves.
	Type of starter
	Recall

Answers

1. 2
2. 5
3. 3
4. 10
5. 9
6. 1
7. 4
8. 8
9. 7
10. 6

Demonstrate with six children. Halve the group, making two groups of three, to remind the class that half of 6 is 3.

Say: *6 divided by 2 is 3. 6 shared out into 2 groups is 3.* Put the two groups back together to show that double 3 is 6.

Practise (with or without groups of children):

1. half of 4
2. half of 10
3. half of 6
4. half of 20
5. half of 18

6. half of 2
7. half of 8
8. half of 16
9. half of 14
10. half of 12

(40) Double and halve

Resources	Learning objective
A board or flipchart	Understand that halving is the inverse of doubling and derive and recall doubles of all numbers to 20, and the corresponding halves.
	Type of starter
	Recall
	Mental strategies
	After two circuits, ask individuals to say the double of any number they choose. Write it outside the circle, next to the number. When this outer circle is complete, say the halves of the outer numbers together. Erase the inner numbers for a last circuit, if appropriate.

No set answers

Draw a clock face as shown.

Ask the children to say the double of each number, in turn, together (for example: 'double 8 is 16').

Visualise

Learning objective	Resources
Visualise common 3D solids; identify shapes from pictures of them in different positions and orientations; sort, make and describe shapes, referring to their properties. **Type of starter** Rehearse	3D shapes: cube, cuboid, sphere, cone, cylinder, pyramid; whiteboards and pens

Describe one of the shapes using the shape properties, number and shape of faces and number of edges and corners.

Ask the children to make a picture in their minds of the shape that you are describing and to think of something in real life that is that shape.

Once they have done this, ask them to draw what they see in their minds on their whiteboards.

Ask them to show their pictures and to describe what they are to a partner or the class.

Repeat for all the shapes. Which were easy to draw as 3D shapes, which were more difficult? Why?

No set answers

 # Draw me!

Learning objective	Resources
Visualise common 2D shapes; identify shapes from pictures of them in different positions and orientations; sort, make and describe shapes, referring to their properties. **Type of starter** Reason	2D shape cards (from photocopiable page 91); whiteboards and pens

Place the 2D shape cards in a pile. Invite a child to come to the front and pick one. They need to describe the shape in terms of its number of sides and corners and number of lines of symmetry.

The rest of the class need to draw the shape that they think the child is describing.

Once they have done this, they show each other their drawing and compare it to the shape being described - is it exactly the same, and if not, what is the same and what is different?

Repeat, with different children describing.

No set answers

BLOCK C

Unit 1

100 Mental Maths Starters				100 Maths Lessons		
Page	Objective	Activity title	Starter type	Unit	Lesson	Page
40	Use lists, tables and diagrams to sort objects; explain choices using appropriate language, including 'not'.	43 Tally ho!	Read	1	2	98, 99
41	Use lists, tables and diagrams to sort objects; explain choices using appropriate language, including 'not'.	44 The shape box	Read	1	3	99
42	Estimate, compare and measure lengths, choosing and using standard units (m, cm) and suitable measuring instruments.	45 Worms!	Rehearse	1	5	100, 101
42	Estimate, compare and measure weights, choosing and using standard units (kg) and suitable measuring instruments.	46 Which is the heaviest?	Rehearse	1	9	104, 105
43	Estimate, compare and measure lengths, weights and capacities, choosing and using standard units (m, cm, kg, litre) and suitable measuring instruments.	47 Which unit?	Reason	1	10	105
44	Read the numbered divisions on a scale, and interpret the divisions between them.	48 Read this	Read	1	7	102, 103

Unit 2

100 Mental Maths Starters				100 Maths Lessons		
Page	Objective	Activity title	Starter type	Unit	Lesson	Page
44	Use lists, tables and diagrams to sort objects; explain choices using appropriate language, including 'not'.	49 Sort it!	Reason	2	1	109, 110
45	Use lists, tables and diagrams to sort objects; explain choices using appropriate language, including 'not'.	50 Land or sea?	Read	2	2	110
46	Use lists, tables and diagrams to sort objects; explain choices using appropriate language, including 'not'.	51 Square or not?	Reason	2	4	111
47	Estimate, compare and measure lengths, choosing and using standard units (m, cm) and suitable measuring instruments.	52 How long?	Rehearse	2	7	114
47	Estimate, compare and measure weights, choosing and using standard units (kg) and suitable measuring instruments.	53 Heavier or lighter?	Rehearse	2	8	114, 115

Unit 2 ...continued

100 Mental Maths Starters				100 Maths Lessons		
Page	Objective	Activity title	Starter type	Unit	Lesson	Page
48	Read the numbered divisions on a scale, and interpret the divisions between them (eg on a scale from 0 to 25 with intervals of 1 shown but only the divisions 0, 5, 10, 15 and 20 numbered).	54 Scales	Read	2	10	116

Unit 3

100 Mental Maths Starters				100 Maths Lessons		
Page	Objective	Activity title	Starter type	Unit	Lesson	Page
48	Use lists, tables and diagrams to sort objects; explain choices using appropriate language, including 'not'.	55 Explain this	Reason	3	1	121, 122
49	Use lists, tables and diagrams to sort objects; explain choices using appropriate language, including 'not'.	56 Where does it go?	Reason	3	2	122
49	Use lists, tables and diagrams to sort objects; explain choices using appropriate language, including 'not'.	57 Block graphs	Reason	3	5	123, 124
50	Estimate, compare and measure capacities, choosing and using standard units (litre) and suitable measuring instruments.	58 Capacity	Refine	3	7	125, 126
50	Estimate, compare and measure lengths, weights and capacities, choosing and using standard units (m, cm, kg, litre) and suitable measuring instruments.	59 Units of measure	Reason	3	10	127
51	Read the numbered divisions on a scale, and interpret the divisions between them (eg on a scale from 0 to 25 with intervals of 1 shown but only the divisions 0, 5, 10, 15 and 20 numbered); use a ruler to draw and measure lines to the nearest centimetre.	60 More scales	Rehearse	3	8	128

43 Tally ho!

Resources	
Whiteboards and pens; a board or flipchart	**Learning objective** Use lists, tables and diagrams to sort objects; explain choices using appropriate language, including 'not'. **Type of starter** Read **Mental strategies** When the children answer the tally questions, observe their strategies, asking for their methods. Encourage counting on for 'how many more…' questions and partitioning, adding 10 and adjusting or knowledge of number pairs for additions.

No set answers

Ask the children to give you the names of ten animals. Write them on the board.

Ask them to choose their favourite from the list. Make a tally of their votes.

Ask them to look at the tallies, make a quick estimate of how many they can see for each animal and write that number on their whiteboards. Give them a few seconds.

Together, count the tallies and ask the children to compare the actual numbers and their estimate.

Ask them to order the numbers from least to greatest on a number line that they draw themselves and then circle the odd numbers.

Ask questions from the tally, such as:

- *How many voted for x?*

- *How many more voted for y than x?*

- *Which animal had x votes?*

- *How many voted for y and z?*

- *How many voted altogether?*

- *If 9 more of you decided to vote for z, how many would that be?*

The shape box

Learning objective	Resources
Use lists, tables and diagrams to sort objects; explain choices using appropriate language, including 'not'.	Whiteboards and pens; copies of 'Mr Smith's shape box' pictogram (from photocopiable page 92)

Type of starter
Read

Mental strategy
When they answer the pictogram questions, ask for their strategies. For counting the sides of the pentagons, use this as an opportunity to count in fives and link to tables.

Give pairs or small groups of children a copy of 'Mr Smith's shape box' pictogram and ask them to tell you what it shows.

Discuss the shapes they see, recapping properties of each, including sides, corners, symmetry.

Ask questions from the pictogram:

1. *How many of each shape does Mr Smith have?*

2. *How many more circles are there than squares?*

3. *How many squares and hexagons are there altogether?*

4. *How many sides do all the pentagons have?*

5. *What about the hexagons?*

6. *How many squares/triangles/etc are missing?*

Discuss what they might write on it to help (names of the shapes on the horizontal axis and numbers on the vertical axis). If appropriate, ask them to write the labels on their copy.

Answers

1. Squares 7, triangles 2, circles 12, hexagons 10, pentagons 3

2. 5

3. 17

4. 15

5. 60

6. Squares 8, triangles 13, circles 3, hexagons 5, pentagons 12

BLOCK C

(45) Worms!

Resources	Learning objective
Plasticine; ruler	Estimate, compare and measure lengths, choosing and using standard units (m, cm) and suitable measuring instruments.
	Type of starter Rehearse

No set answers

The children should work in small groups of about four. Each child needs a small lump of plasticine.

Give them 30 seconds to roll the plasticine to make the longest worm that they can. They lie them side-by-side from shortest to longest.

Show a 30cm rule and ask them to use it to estimate the length of the shortest worm and write that down on their whiteboards.

They measure it, compare with their estimate and then use that to estimate the length of the next worm.

Continue until all worms have been estimated and measured.

Ask questions to different groups, such as:

- *Who made the closest estimate?*

- *What is the difference between that and the actual length?*

- *How long was the longest worm?*

- *How much longer was it than the shortest?*

(46) Which is the heaviest?

Resources	Learning objective
Balance scales	Estimate, compare and measure weights, choosing and using standard units (kg) and suitable measuring instruments.
	Type of starter Rehearse

No set answers

The children should work in small groups of about four.

Ask each child to find an object from their table or somewhere in the classroom.

Ask them to feel the weight of each one and order them from heaviest to lightest on their table.

Next, ask them to use the balance to weigh pairs of the items to check whether they have put them in the correct order.

Ask the whole class to:

- stand up if they have the heaviest object in the group

- stand up if they have the lightest object in the group.

(47) **Which unit?**

Learning objective
Estimate, compare and measure lengths, weights and capacities, choosing and using standard units (m, cm, kg, litre) and suitable measuring instruments.

Type of starter
Reason

Resources
Picture cards (cut from photocopiable page 93); whiteboards and pens

The children should sit in a group in front of you with their whiteboards and pens so that they can see the cards as you hold them up.

Invite children to pick a card, and ask the class to tell you what they see.

With the children, recap the meanings of length, weight and capacity and the units of m, cm, kg, litre.

For each card ask:

*   *Would you weigh this, measure its length or find out how much it will hold?*

*   *What unit would you measure this in?*

Ask them to write what they think the answer is on their whiteboards and then show you.

If any child gives an unusual answer, explore it to see what they were thinking. For example: weight for glass of juice – they might be thinking of the glass and not the juice.

Answers

1. Car: weight, kg
2. Swimming pool: capacity, litre
3. String: length, cm or m
4. Cheese: weight, kg
5. Bottle of water: capacity, litre or weight, kg
6. Child: weight, kg or height, cm
7. Bucket: capacity, litre or weight, kg
8. Road: length, m
9. Tree: length/ height, m
10. Bath: capacity, litres

(48) **Read this**

Resources A board or flipchart	**Learning objective** Read the numbered divisions on a scale, and interpret the divisions between them. **Type of starter** Read
No set answers	Draw a ruler on the board with divisions up to 30. Leave it blank and ask the children to tell you where certain numbers should go, beginning with the halfway mark. Target children with specific numbers. Together, fill the ruler. Tell the children that they are going to pretend it is a ruler measuring in pretend centimetres. Ask individuals to draw arrows at points that you call out. Ask individuals to plot their own arrows on the ruler and tell the class where they have placed them. Ask questions, such as: *What number should go two after this division?* Repeat this for a circular weighing scale and a vertical measuring cylinder.

Unit 2

(49) **Sort it!**

Resources A board or flipchart	**Learning objective** Use lists, tables and diagrams to sort objects; explain choices using appropriate language, including 'not'. **Type of starter** Reason
No set answers	Draw a circle on the board. Ask the children to give you numbers to 30. As they do, write the odd numbers inside the circle and the even ones outside. The children need to work out what is special about the numbers inside the circle and then think of an appropriate label to write inside it. Repeat this with other criteria. For example: multiples of 5 or 10, or numbers with a 3 in them. Ask for volunteers to play 'teacher' and make up their own criteria, or give them one if they need the help.

(50) **Land or sea?**

Learning objective Use lists, tables and diagrams to sort objects; explain choices using appropriate language, including 'not'. **Type of starter** Read	**Resources** A board or flipchart

No set answers

Draw a table on the board with two columns headed 'Land' and 'Sea' as shown below.

Ask the children in pairs to think of some items that could go in each column, for example: house, elephant on land; boat, fish in the sea.

Invite them to share their suggestions.

Then ask the class to decide the best place on the table to put their suggested items and to give reasons why.

Encourage discussion when appropriate.

Land	Sea
Elephant	Boat
House	Fish

(51) Square or not?

Resources

3D shapes: sphere, cube, pyramid, cuboids (one with six rectangular faces and one with two square faces and four rectangular), cone, cylinder; bag

Answers

Square face: cube, cuboid, pyramid

No square face: sphere, cuboid, cone, cylinder

Learning objective

Use lists, tables and diagrams to sort objects; explain choices using appropriate language, including 'not'.

Type of starter

Reason

Draw a simple Carroll diagram on the board with two columns, one headed 'Square face' and the other 'No square face' as shown below.

Show the 3D shapes, discuss their names and properties.

Put the 3D shapes into a bag.

Invite children to take a shape out of the bag, name and describe it to everyone.

As a class, agree where on the table it should go and give the reason why.

Square face	No square face

(52) How long?

Learning objective	Resources
Estimate, compare and measure lengths, choosing and using standard units (m, cm) and suitable measuring instruments.	Metre stick; ruler; items from the classroom; whiteboards and pens
Type of starter Rehearse	

Show the children a metre stick and a 30cm ruler.

Choose various classroom items that are: longer than the metre stick (for example, table top, door); shorter than the metre stick but longer than the ruler (for example, large book); shorter than the ruler (for example, pencil).

Ask the children to stand. Show or point to the items one at a time. They need to decide which category the items fall into. Say: *If the item is longer than a metre, put your arms in the air and clap. If it's in between, clap in front of you. If it's shorter than the ruler, touch the floor.*

Extend this by encouraging them to estimate how long they think the item is, write it on their whiteboards and then together measure to see how close they are.

No set answers

(53) Heavier or lighter?

Learning objective	Resources
Estimate, compare and measure weights, choosing and using standard units (kg) and suitable measuring instruments.	Balance scales; kitchen scales; 1kg bag of sugar; items from the classroom; whiteboards and pens
Type of starter Rehearse	

Ask the children to choose one item from the classroom and then to stand in a circle, if possible, with their item.

Pass the bag of sugar round the class, after informing them that it weighs 1kg. They compare the weight of their item with the bag of sugar. If they think it is lighter, they sit down.

Ask any child that remains standing to measure their item against the bag of sugar on the balance scales, if possible, to check that they are right.

Ask the children what they would need to find out the exact weight. Establish that they would need scales with divisions.

Choose a few children who are sitting to weigh their items to get the exact weight.

No set answers

BLOCK C

(54) Scales

Resources	Learning objective
A board or flipchart	Read the numbered divisions on a scale, and interpret the divisions between them (eg on a scale from 0 to 25 with intervals of 1 shown but only the divisions 0, 5, 10, 15 and 20 numbered).
	Type of starter
	Read

No set answers

Draw a thermometer on the board with a scale of divisions to 30. Make every second division longer than the others. Tell the children that they are going to pretend these are degrees Celsius. Ask them to count in twos and, as they do, you mark every other division, beginning at zero.

Invite children to plot on different temperatures, include marked and unmarked divisions.

Discuss whether the temperatures are cold, cool, warm or hot. Ask children to make up an action to do for each.

Point at some of the temperatures the children marked on and ask the children to do the action they made up to signify whether that temperature is cold, cool, warm or hot.

To extend, adjust the thermometer so that the temperatures go to -10.

(55) Explain this

Resources	Learning objective
A board or flipchart	Use lists, tables and diagrams to sort objects; explain choices using appropriate language, including 'not'.
	Type of starter
	Reason
	Mental strategy
	Look for suggestions to do with number of sides, corners and whether the shapes are symmetrical.

No set answers

Draw two circles on the board. In one, draw a circle, an ellipse, a triangle, a square and a rectangle with at least one line of symmetry. In the second, draw two irregular pentagons, hexagons and octagons. Ensure that these have no symmetry.

Ask the children to identify the shapes and tell you their properties (including sides, corners and symmetry).

Ask them to look at your diagram and to think of headings they could use to describe what is in each circle without using the shape names.

Take feedback, aiming for suggestions such as 'four sides or less', 'more than four sides', 'symmetrical', 'not symmetrical'. Expect them to explain any reasons for their suggestions.

(56) **Where does it go?**

Learning objective
Use lists, tables and diagrams to sort objects; explain choices using appropriate language, including 'not'.

Type of starter
Reason

Mental strategy
Observe how they stick their sticky notes on the board: do they group them according to shapes that are the same, or do they randomly place them on the board? If the latter, discuss how they could position them to make it easy for you to find out how many of each there are.

Resources
Sticky notes or similar; a board or flipchart

Give each child a sticky note and ask them to draw a 2D shape on it.

Tell them that they will be sticking their shapes on the board so you can see how many of each shape have been drawn. Ask them to think about how they should display their shapes.

Invite the children in groups of four to come to the front and stick their shapes on the board.

Aim towards the final result being a pictogram. Ask them to help you label the axes of the pictogram and make up a title.

Finish by asking questions to identify the numbers of each shape and also how many more/less/altogether.

No set answers

(57) **Block graphs**

Learning objective
Use lists, tables and diagrams to sort objects; explain choices using appropriate language, including 'not'.

Type of starter
Reason

Mental strategy
Don't give instructions about how to draw a block graph: let them have a go!

Resources
Multilink cubes of four different colours; whiteboards and pens; a board or flipchart

Place a selection of the four colours of cubes on each table. Ask the children to pick their favourite colour cube.

Next, ask them in groups to come to the front and give you their cube. Ask them how they could arrange these so that it will be easy for everyone to see which the most popular colour is. Invite volunteers to arrange them accordingly. Aim for towers.

Ask questions about the towers, for example: *Which is the most/least popular colour? How many more like x than y? How many like x and y?*

Next, ask them to draw a block graph of this on their whiteboards. Show a few of the results and then draw one of your own on the board. Ask them to compare theirs with yours and assess how they did.

No set answers

BLOCK C

(58) Capacity

Resources Three 2-litre bottles; a 1-litre measuring jug; water	**Learning objective** Estimate, compare and measure capacities, choosing and using standard units (litre) and suitable measuring instruments. **Type of starter** Refine

No set answers

Hold up one of the empty bottles, explain that it holds 2 litres and say you want to half fill it. Ask: *How much will that be?* Start filling the bottle and ask the children to say 'stop' when they think there is 1 litre in it.

Next, say that you want to fill the second bottle so that there is half the amount you have just made. Ask: *How much will that be?* Expect the children to tell you half a litre (some may be able to tell you 500ml). Start filling and ask them to say 'stop' when they think there is half a litre in it.

Now, say you want to fill the third bottle so it is halfway between 1 litre and 2 litres. Ask: *How much will that be?* Expect them to tell you 1½ litres. Ask for another way of saying this (1.5 litres or 1500ml). Start filling and ask them to say 'stop' when they think there is 1½ litres in it.

Finally, invite volunteers to help you check each bottle to find how close their estimates were.

(59) Units of measure

Resources Selection of objects from around the classroom; containers such as mug, glass, bowl; whiteboards and pens	**Learning objective** Estimate, compare and measure lengths, weights and capacities, choosing and using standard units (m, cm, kg, litre) and suitable measuring instruments. **Type of starter** Reason

No set answers

Recap the meanings of length, weight and capacity, how each would be measured and the appropriate units: m, cm, kg, litre.

Show each of the objects and containers in turn. Ask the children to write on the whiteboards the unit in which each would be measured, and then to show you.

For example, hold up a bowl and say:

- *In what unit would you measure its weight?*
- *In what unit would you measure its height?*
- *What unit would you use to measure the amount of water it would hold?*

For each, ask them to explain why they wrote their chosen unit.

(60) **More scales**

Learning objective	Resources
Read the numbered divisions on a scale, and interpret the divisions between them (eg on a scale from 0 to 25 with intervals of 1 shown but only the divisions 0, 5, 10, 15 and 20 numbered); use a ruler to draw and measure lines to the nearest centimetre.	Metre stick with coloured 10cm sections

Type of starter
Rehearse

No set answers

Show the metre stick, using the side with the 10cm coloured sections and no numbers (if you do not have one of these, you could use a counting stick of the same or similar length). Tell the children that this is a scale that goes from 0 to 100cm.

Point to the ten divisions and ask them how many centimetres they think each section between the divisions is worth. Establish that each is 10cm.

Together, count in tens from the 0 position to the 100cm mark, pointing at each division as you do so.

Repeat this but jump backwards and forwards, skipping sections at times.

Next, point at positions halfway between the divisions, for example: 25cm, 65cm. Ask: *Can you work out what length that would be?*

Place your finger just in front or after the divisions and ask them to estimate what would be there, for example: 21cm, 49cm.

BLOCK D

Unit 1

	100 Mental Maths Starters				100 Maths Lessons		
Page	Objective	Activity title	Starter type	Unit	Lesson	Page
54	Solve problems involving addition, subtraction, multiplication or division in contexts of numbers, measures or pounds and pence.	**61** Money, money, money	Read	1	4	138
54	Use practical and informal written methods to add and subtract two-digit numbers.	**62** Adding: grouping tens and units	Refresh	1	1	135, 136
55	Add or subtract mentally a one-digit number or a multiple of 10 to or from any two-digit number; use practical and informal written methods to add and subtract two-digit numbers.	**63** Subtraction to 20	Refine	1	2	136
55	Estimate, compare and measure lengths, choosing and using standard units (m, cm) and suitable measuring instruments.	**64** Metre or centimetre?	Reason	1	7	140
56	Use units of time (seconds, minutes, hours, days) and know the relationships between them; read the time to the quarter hour; identify time intervals, including those that cross the hour.	**65** One hour later and earlier	Rehearse	1	8	140, 141
57	Use units of time (seconds, minutes, hours, days) and know the relationships between them; read the time to the quarter hour; identify time intervals, including those that cross the hour.	**66** Later and earlier	Rehearse	1	9	141

Unit 2

	100 Mental Maths Starters				100 Maths Lessons		
Page	Objective	Activity title	Starter type	Unit	Lesson	Page
58	Solve problems involving addition, subtraction, multiplication or division in contexts of numbers, measures or pounds and pence.	**67** Pounds or pence?	Read	2	1	147, 148
59	Add or subtract mentally a one-digit number or a multiple of 10 to or from any two-digit number; use practical and informal written methods to add and subtract two-digit numbers.	**68** Near doubles	Refine	2	2	148
60	Estimate, compare and measure weights, choosing and using standard units (kg) and suitable measuring instruments.	**69** More or less than a kilogram?	Reason	2	7	152

Unit 2 ...continued

	100 Mental Maths Starters			100 Maths Lessons		
Page	Objective	Activity title	Starter type	Unit	Lesson	Page
61	Use units of time (seconds, minutes, hours, days) and know the relationships between them; read the time to the quarter hour; identify time intervals, including those that cross the hour.	70 Three hours later and earlier	Rehearse	2	8	152
62	Use units of time (seconds, minutes, hours, days) and know the relationships between them; read the time to the quarter hour; identify time intervals, including those that cross the hour.	71 Quarter to: two hours later and earlier	Rehearse	2	9	153
62	Follow and give instructions involving position, direction and movement.	72 Where is it?	Read	2	10	154

Unit 3

	100 Mental Maths Starters			100 Maths Lessons		
Page	Objective	Activity title	Starter type	Unit	Lesson	Page
63	Add or subtract mentally a one-digit number or a multiple of 10 to or from any two-digit number; use practical and informal written methods to add and subtract two-digit numbers.	73 Adding two-digit numbers	Rehearse	3	1	159, 160
64	Add mentally a one-digit number or a multiple of 10 to any two-digit number; use practical and informal written methods to add two-digit numbers.	74 Add it!	Refine	3	2	160
64	Estimate, compare and measure capacities, choosing and using standard units (litre) and suitable measuring instruments.	75 More or less than a litre?	Reason	3	5	163, 164
65	Use units of time (seconds, minutes, hours, days) and know the relationships between them; identify time intervals, including those that cross the hour.	76 Half past: two hours later and earlier	Rehearse	3	6	164
66	Use units of time (seconds, minutes, hours, days) and know the relationships between them; read the time to the quarter hour; identify time intervals, including those that cross the hour.	77 How many minutes?	Recall	3	7	165
67	Use units of time (seconds, minutes, hours, days) and know the relationships between them; read the time to the quarter hour; identify time intervals, including those that cross the hour.	78 Time intervals	Rehearse	3	10	167

BLOCK D

⑥¹ **Money, money, money**

Resources	Learning objective
Whiteboards and pens; a board or flipchart	Solve problems involving addition, subtraction, multiplication or division in contexts of numbers, measures or pounds and pence.
	Type of starter
	Read

No set answers

Ask the children to think of some three-digit numbers and to write them on their whiteboards.

Next, ask the children to read their numbers to a neighbour and then show you. Select six numbers to write on the board.

Tell the children that they are going to pretend these numbers are in pennies. Recap how many pennies in a pound, then ask children to convert the pennies into £p notation (for example: 247 becomes £2.47) and to read the amount correctly. Repeat this a few times.

Say some money amounts (for example: £6.98, £1.74, £3.08) and ask them to write these as pennies.

⑥² **Adding: grouping tens and units**

Resources	Learning objective
A board or flipchart	Use practical and informal written methods to add and subtract two-digit numbers.
	Type of starter
	Refresh
	Mental strategy
	Encourage the children to group together the tens first, then add the ones. For example: 23 + 14 = 20 + 10 + 3 + 4 = 30 + 3 + 4 = 37.

Answers

1. 38
2. 46
3. 39
4. 48
5. 36
6. 47
7. 27
8. 49

Write: 23 + 14 =

Ask for the answer and the methods used to find it.

Write each addition sentence. Give the children time to work it out. Ask a child to say the answer and (if possible) explain the method used.

1.	25 + 13	5.	13 + 23
2.	32 + 14	6.	35 + 12
3.	14 + 25	7.	13 + 14
4.	31 + 17	8.	16 + 33

(63) **Subtraction to 20**

Learning objective
Add or subtract mentally a one-digit number or a multiple of 10 to or from any two-digit number; use practical and informal written methods to add and subtract two-digit numbers.

Type of starter
Refine

Resources
Two PE hoops; a set of numeral cards 0–20 (from photocopiable pages 85 and 86)

No set answers

Sit the children in a semi-circle facing the two hoops. Ask the first two children to stand in separate hoops, take a card from the shuffled set, then show and say the number.

Ask a third child to subtract one number from the other and (if possible) explain the method used. For example:

- 14 – 11 = 3: counting on from the smaller to the larger number

- 15 – 7 = 8: using complementary addition and pairs that make 10 (15 = 7 + 3 + 5, so 15 – 7 = 3 + 5 = 8).

(64) **Metre or centimetre?**

Learning objective
Estimate, compare and measure lengths, choosing and using standard units (m, cm) and suitable measuring instruments.

Type of starter
Reason

Resources
Items from the classroom; classroom ruler; metre stick; whiteboards and pens

No set answers

Show the children the ruler and ask them to write on their whiteboard the shorthand for the measurements that can be made on it, for example: cm. Do any write mm? If so, explore what they think this means.

Repeat with the metre stick.

Hold up different items from the classroom or point to things on the wall or floor. The children should write the abbreviation for the unit they think the items should be measured in.

Extend this into an activity where they estimate the length of the items. Together, measure the actual length and ask them to work out how close their estimates were.

BLOCK D

(65) # One hour later and earlier

Resources	Learning objective
A teaching clock	Use units of time (seconds, minutes, hours, days) and know the relationships between them; read the time to the quarter hour; identify time intervals, including those that cross the hour.

Type of starter
Rehearse

Answers

1. 8 o'clock
2. 4 o'clock
3. 6 o'clock
4. 1 o'clock
5. 9 o'clock
6. 5 o'clock
7. 2 o'clock
8. 11 o'clock

9. 5 o'clock
10. 8 o'clock
11. 3 o'clock
12. 1 o'clock
13. 10 o'clock
14. 12 o'clock
15. 6 o'clock
16. 2 o'clock

Sit the children in a circle, facing the teaching clock. Set the hands on the clock to show 10 o'clock. Ask: *What time is being shown?*

Choose a child to say the time one hour later.

Ask individuals for the time one hour later than:

1. 7 o'clock

2. 3 o'clock

3. 5 o'clock

4. 12 o'clock

5. 8 o'clock

6. 4 o'clock

7. 1 o'clock

8. 10 o'clock

Ask individuals for the time one hour earlier than:

9. 6 o'clock

10. 9 o'clock

11. 4 o'clock

12. 2 o'clock

13. 11 o'clock

14. 1 o'clock

15. 7 o'clock

16. 3 o'clock

(66) Later and earlier

Learning objective
Use units of time (seconds, minutes, hours, days) and know the relationships between them; read the time to the quarter hour; identify time intervals, including those that cross the hour.

Type of starter
Rehearse

Mental strategies
Before asking question 9, show half past nine on the clock and remind the class of the position of both hands.

Resources
A teaching clock

Ask the children to say the time shown on the clock and the time two hours later. Children raise a hand to answer.

1. 5 o'clock

2. 2 o'clock

3. 12 o'clock

4. 8 o'clock

5. 4 o'clock

6. 11 o'clock

7. 6 o'clock

8. 1 o'clock

For the remaining questions, ask the children to say the time shown and the time one hour later.

9. half past 8

10. half past 5

11. half past 1

12. half past 10

13. half past 3

14. half past 12

15. half past 6

16. half past 2

Answers

1. 7 o'clock
2. 4 o'clock
3. 2 o'clock
4. 10 o'clock
5. 6 o'clock
6. 1 o'clock
7. 8 o'clock
8. 3 o'clock

9. half past 9
10. half past 6
11. half past 2
12. half past 11
13. half past 4
14. half past 1
15. half past 7
16. half past 3

---

(67) **Pounds or pence?**

Resources Two sets of cards (from photocopiable page 94); whiteboards and pens	**Learning objective** Solve problems involving addition, subtraction, multiplication or division in contexts of numbers, measures or pounds and pence. **Type of starter** Read

No set answers

Give a card to each child.

Ask them to read it to a partner and then write it on their whiteboard, both in pennies and in £p notation.

Their partner should check to see if they agree.

Invite five children to come to the front and show their cards. Ensure that these children have a mix of pennies and £p notation cards. They should read them in both notations.

Ask the class to order the cards that these children are holding from the smallest to greatest amount.

Near doubles

Learning objective Add or subtract mentally a one-digit number or a multiple of 10 to or from any two-digit number; use practical and informal written methods to add and subtract two-digit numbers. **Type of starter** Refine	**Resources** A board or flipchart

Remind the children how to use doubles they know to help them add together numbers that are almost the same.

Write:

$$7 + 8 = 14 + 1 = 15$$

Say: *Double the lower number and add one.*

Children raise a hand to answer:

1.   5 + 6

2.   10 + 11

3.   20 + 21

4.   8 + 9

5.   3 + 4

Write:

$$7 + 8 = 14 + 1 = 15$$

Ask an individual to explain how this differs from the previous examples (doubling the higher number and taking away one).

Children raise a hand to answer:

6.   5 + 4

7.   7 + 6

8.   12 + 11

9.   29 + 30

10.   15 + 14

Answers

1.   11
2.   21
3.   41
4.   17
5.   7

6.   9
7.   13
8.   23
9.   59
10. 29

(69) More or less than a kilogram?

Resources	Learning objective
Items from the classroom; something the children are familiar with that weighs 1kg (for example: bag of sugar or potatoes); balance scales; whiteboards and pens	Estimate, compare and measure weights, choosing and using standard units (kg) and suitable measuring instruments. **Type of starter** Reason

No set answers

Show the children the bag of sugar or potatoes. Ask them to tell you how much they think it weighs.

Establish that it is 1kg, weighing it on scales if you wish. Ask them to write that amount on their whiteboard.

Ask the children to draw the 'greater than' (>) and 'less than' (<) symbols on their boards. Remind them what they look like if necessary.

Pick up your chosen items and ask the children to write the correct symbol to show if they think the item is heavier or lighter than 1kg.

For each, weigh the item on the balance scales to check the children's responses.

(70) Three hours later and earlier

Learning objective	Resources
Use units of time (seconds, minutes, hours, days) and know the relationships between them; read the time to the quarter hour; identify time intervals, including those that cross the hour.	A teaching clock

Type of starter
Rehearse

Explain that you are going to show an 'o'clock' time.

The children raise a hand to say the time that the clock shows and the time three hours later.

1. 6 o'clock

2. 2 o'clock

3. 8 o'clock

4. 3 o'clock

5. 7 o'clock

6. 11 o'clock

7. 5 o'clock

8. 10 o'clock

For the remaining questions, ask the children to say the time shown and the time three hours earlier.

9. 9 o'clock

10. 11 o'clock

11. 5 o'clock

12. 8 o'clock

13. 3 o'clock

14. 1 o'clock

15. 7 o'clock

16. 2 o'clock

Answers

1. 9 o'clock
2. 5 o'clock
3. 11 o'clock
4. 6 o'clock
5. 10 o'clock
6. 2 o'clock
7. 8 o'clock
8. 1 o'clock

9. 6 o'clock
10. 8 o'clock
11. 2 o'clock
12. 5 o'clock
13. 12 o'clock
14. 10 o'clock
15. 4 o'clock
16. 11 o'clock

(71) Quarter to: two hours later and earlier

| **Resources**
A teaching clock | **Learning objective**
Use units of time (seconds, minutes, hours, days) and know the relationships between them; read the time to the quarter hour; identify time intervals, including those that cross the hour.

Type of starter
Rehearse |

Answers

1. quarter to 4
2. quarter to 7
3. quarter to 3
4. quarter to 8
5. quarter to 1
6. quarter to 5
7. quarter to 2
8. quarter to 9
9. quarter to 6
10. quarter to 11
11. quarter to 12
12. quarter to 10

Sit the children in a semicircle, facing the teaching clock.

Ask them to say the 'quarter to' time shown on the clock and the time two hours later.

1. quarter to 2
2. quarter to 5
3. quarter to 1

4. quarter to 6
5. quarter to 11
6. quarter to 3

For the following questions, ask them to say the time shown and the time two hours earlier.

7. quarter to 4
8. quarter to 11
9. quarter to 8

10. quarter to 1
11. quarter to 2
12. quarter to 12

(72) Where is it?

| **Resources**
Photocopiable page 95 displayed on a whiteboard; whiteboards and pens | **Learning objective**
Follow and give instructions involving position, direction and movement.

Type of starter
Read

Mental strategy
Remind the children if necessary that the coordinates are read horizontally first. |

Answers

Squares (5): A1, A7, B4, D5, D7, F8

Circles (6): A3, A6, B8, C6, D1, E3

Triangles (4): B2, D3, E6, F1

Pentagons (5): A5, C1, C4, E2, F6

Display photocopiable page 95 on the whiteboard.

Ask the children to identify the shapes that they can see and to rehearse the properties of these shapes, including the number of sides and corners and any lines of symmetry. Ask them to count how many there are of each shape.

Ask them to tell you how to identify the position of the shapes on the grid.

Ask them to write the coordinates for the squares on their whiteboards, then the coordinates for the circles, triangles and pentagons.

Adding two-digit numbers

Learning objective	Resources
Add or subtract mentally a one-digit number or a multiple of 10 to or from any two-digit number; use practical and informal written methods to add and subtract two-digit numbers.	A board or flipchart
Type of starter Rehearse	

Write:

13 + 36 =

Tell the children that they have to decide what to do.

They can:

*   put the largest number first, then count on in tens and ones, 36 + 13 = 36 + 10 + 3 = 46 + 3 = 49 or 49.

Or, they can:

*   split the two numbers into tens and ones, add the tens, then add on the ones, 13 + 36 = 10 + 3 + 30 + 6 = 40 + 3 + 6 = 49.

Children put up a hand to answer the questions. Ask each child to explain the method they used.

Write each example in turn.

1.   23 + 14

2.   17 + 22

3.   35 + 15

4.   26 + 23

5.   13 + 38

6.   21 + 35

Answers
1.   37
2.   39
3.   50
4.   49
5.   51
6.   56

BLOCK D

(74) Add it!

Resources
Whiteboards and pens; a board or flipchart

Learning objective
Add mentally a one-digit number or a multiple of 10 to any two-digit number; use practical and informal written methods to add two-digit numbers.

Type of starter
Refine

Mental strategies
Near doubles; number pairs to 10; bridging 10; rounding to nearest 10 and adjusting.

Ask for volunteers to share their strategies. Focus on the one intended (for example: bridging 10) and then repeat additions asking the children to use that strategy.

No set answers

Write on the board different numbers for the children to add together.

You need to encourage the following strategies.

- Near doubles, for example: 5 + 6, 12 + 13.

- Number pairs to 10, for example: 2 + 8, 21 + 9.

- Bridging 10, for example: 18 + 7.

- Rounding to nearest 10 and adjusting, for example: 15 + 9, 35 + 19.

For each one, they write their answer on their whiteboard.

(75) More or less than a litre?

Resources
Different containers from around the classroom; 1-litre bottle of water; measuring jug; whiteboards and pens

Learning objective
Estimate, compare and measure capacities, choosing and using standard units (litre) and suitable measuring instruments.

Type of starter
Reason

No set answers

Show the children the bottle of water. Ask them to tell you how much they think is in it. Establish that it is 1 litre using the measuring jug.

Ask them to draw the 'greater than' (>) and 'less than' (<) symbols on their boards. Remind them what they look like if necessary.

Pick up your chosen items and ask them to write the correct symbol to show if they think it would contain more or less than 1 litre.

For each, pour the water from the bottle into the container to check.

76 Half past: two hours later and earlier

Learning objective Use units of time (seconds, minutes, hours, days) and know the relationships between them; identify time intervals, including those that cross the hour. **Type of starter** Rehearse	**Resources** A teaching clock

Sit the children in a semicircle, facing the teaching clock.

Ask them to say the 'half past' time shown on the clock and the time two hours later.

1. half past 9

2. half past 2

3. half past 7

4. half past 4

5. half past 11

6. half past 8

7. half past 1

8. half past 10

For the following questions, ask the children to say the time shown and the time two hours earlier.

9. half past 12

10. half past 3

11. half past 9

12. half past 5

13. half past 1

14. half past 7

15. half past 2

16. half past 6

Answers

1. half past 11
2. half past 4
3. half past 9
4. half past 6
5. half past 1
6. half past 10
7. half past 3
8. half past 12

9. half past 10
10. half past 1
11. half past 7
12. half past 3
13. half past 11
14. half past 5
15. half past 12
16. half past 4

(77) **How many minutes?**

Resources Whiteboards and pens	**Learning objective** Use units of time (seconds, minutes, hours, days) and know the relationships between them; read the time to the quarter hour; identify time intervals, including those that cross the hour.
	Type of starter Recall
	Mental strategies Use known facts.
	Aim their thinking towards, for example: if they know 3 × 6 is 18, then 3 × 60 is 180.

Answers

1. 60, 120, 180, 300, 600

2. 30, 15, 45

Ask the children to write the answers to these questions on their whiteboards.

1. How many minutes are there in an hour? Two hours? Three hours? Five hours? Ten hours? How do you know?

2. How many minutes in half an hour? One quarter of an hour? Three quarters of an hour?

Next, call out some numbers of minutes and ask the children to work out and write down how many hours and minutes they are, for example: 65 minutes, 70 minutes, 75 minutes.

Share a common strategy for doing this, for example: taking away 60, as that is one hour; the number left will be the minutes.

(78) Time intervals

Learning objective
Use units of time (seconds, minutes, hours, days) and know the relationships between them; read the time to the quarter hour; identify time intervals, including those that cross the hour.

Type of starter
Rehearse

Resources
Whiteboards and pens; individual clocks

Ask the children to write on their whiteboards the answers to these (and similar) problems. Let the children use their clocks to help them.

1. How many minutes between half past 3 and 3:45?

2. I began reading at a quarter to 10 and finished at five past. For how long did I read?

3. Sam left home to go to the shops at 2 o'clock. He came back at 4:30. How long was he away from home?

4. The farmer started milking his cows at 6 o'clock and he finished at 7:15. For how long was he milking them?

Once you have asked a few questions, ask the children to make up some more story problems to ask a partner.

Invite volunteers to ask their problems to the class for them to answer.

Answers
1. 15 minutes
2. 20 minutes
3. 2½ hours
4. 1 hour 15 minutes

BLOCK E

Unit 1

	100 Mental Maths Starters			100 Maths Lessons		
Page	Objective	Activity title	Starter type	Unit	Lesson	Page
70	Represent repeated sharing and repeated subtraction (grouping) as division; use practical and informal written methods and related vocabulary to support multiplication and division, including calculations with remainders.	79 Grouping	Rehearse	1	6	175, 176
70	Use the symbols '+', '−', '×', '÷' and '=' to record and interpret number sentences involving all four operations; calculate the value of an unknown in a number sentence (eg □ ÷ 2 = 6, 30 − □ = 24).	80 What's missing?	Rehearse	1	8	177
71	Use the symbols '+', '−', '×', '÷' and '=' to record and interpret number sentences involving all four operations; calculate the value of an unknown in a number sentence (eg □ ÷ 2 = 6, 30 − □ = 24).	81 What's missing now?	Rehearse	1	9	177, 178
71	Derive and recall doubles of all numbers to 20, and the corresponding halves.	82 Doubles and halves	Recall	1	10	178
72	Derive and recall multiplication facts for the two-times table and the related division facts; recognise multiples of 2.	83 Two-times table facts	Recall	1	2	172, 173
73	Derive and recall multiplication facts for the two- and ten-times table and the related division facts; recognise multiples of 2 and 10.	84 Two- and ten-times tables	Recall	1	3	173
74	Derive and recall multiplication facts for the five-times table and the related division facts; recognise multiples of 5.	85 Counting in fives	Refine	1	5	174, 175
74	Find one-half, one-quarter and three-quarters of shapes and sets of objects.	86 Not all there!	Rehearse	1	15	181

Unit 2

	100 Mental Maths Starters			100 Maths Lessons		
Page	Objective	Activity title	Starter type	Unit	Lesson	Page
75	Solve problems involving addition, subtraction, multiplication or division in contexts of numbers, measures or pounds and pence.	87 Multiple buying	Rehearse	2	2	190
76	Represent repeated addition and arrays as multiplication, and sharing and repeated subtraction (grouping) as division; use practical and informal written methods and related vocabulary to support multiplication and division, including calculations with remainders.	88 Arrays	Read	2	4	192

Unit 2 ...continued

100 Mental Maths Starters				100 Maths Lessons		
Page	Objective	Activity title	Starter type	Unit	Lesson	Page
76	Understand that halving is the inverse of doubling and derive and recall doubles of all numbers to 20, and the corresponding halves.	89 Double that!	Recall	2	11	198
77	Derive and recall multiplication facts for the two-times table; recognise multiples of 2.	90 Two-times table practice	Recall	2	6	193, 194
78	Derive and recall multiplication facts for the ten-times table and the related division facts; recognise multiples of 10.	91 Ten-times table facts	Recall	2	7	194
79	Derive and recall multiplication facts for the five-times table and the related division facts; recognise multiples of 5.	92 Times 5	Recall	2	8	195, 196
79	Derive and recall multiplication facts for the two-, five- and ten-times tables and the related division facts; recognise multiples of 2, 5 and 10.	93 Multiples	Refine	2	12	198, 199
80	Find one-half, one-quarter and three-quarters of shapes and sets of objects.	94 What fraction?	Rehearse	2	15	200

Unit 3

100 Mental Maths Starters				100 Maths Lessons		
Page	Objective	Activity title	Starter type	Unit	Lesson	Page
80	Solve problems involving addition, subtraction, multiplication or division in contexts of numbers, measures or pounds and pence.	95 Multiple shopping	Rehearse	3	9	213
81	Represent repeated addition and arrays as multiplication, and sharing and repeated subtraction (grouping) as division; use practical and informal written methods and related vocabulary to support multiplication and division, including calculations with remainders.	96 More arrays	Read	3	6	211
82	Understand that halving is the inverse of doubling and derive and recall doubles of all numbers to 20, and the corresponding halves.	97 Doubles and halves	Recall	3	14	216, 217
82	Derive and recall multiplication facts for the two-times table and the related division facts; recognise multiples of 2.	98 Times 2, divided by 2	Recall	3	5	211
83	Derive and recall multiplication facts for the two- and ten-times tables and the related division facts; recognise multiples of 2 and 10.	99 Times 2 and times 10	Recall	3	6	211
83	Derive and recall multiplication facts for the two-, five- and ten-times tables and the related division facts; recognise multiples of 2, 5 and 10.	100 Two-, five- and ten-times tables	Recall	3	7	212
84	Derive and recall multiplication facts for the two-, five- and ten-times tables and the related division facts; recognise multiples of 2, 5 and 10.	101 Count on and count back	Refine	3	11	215
84	Find one-half, one-quarter and three-quarters of shapes and sets of objects.	102 Fractions of numbers	Rehearse	3	15	217

(79) **Grouping**

Resources
Whiteboards and pens; piles of 30 counters, or similar, per pair

Learning objective
Represent repeated sharing and repeated subtraction (grouping) as division; use practical and informal written methods and related vocabulary to support multiplication and division, including calculations with remainders.

Type of starter
Rehearse

Answers
24 ÷ 9 = 2 with 6 left over

Possible answers:
24 ÷ 2 = 12

24 ÷ 3 = 8

24 ÷ 4 = 6

24 ÷ 6 = 4

24 ÷ 8 = 3

24 ÷ 12 = 2

Briefly ask the children what they think is meant by dividing and grouping. Ask them to write the division symbol.

Ask the children to work in pairs, take 10 counters and group them into twos. Ask: *How many groups are there?* Ask them to write a number sentence to show this (10 ÷ 2 = 5). Repeat this with a variety of even numbers up to 20.

Ask them to take 30 counters, group them in twos, threes, fives and tens and write the appropriate number sentences (for example: 30 ÷ 2 = 15).

Ask them to take 24 counters and group them into piles of nine. Ask: *How many groups are there? How many will be left over?* Now, ask them to group them so that there are none left (see possible answers). How many different solutions did they find?

(80) **What's missing?**

Resources
Whiteboards and pens; piles of 30 counters, or similar, per pair

Learning objective
Use the symbols '+', '–', '×', '÷' and '=' to record and interpret number sentences involving all four operations; calculate the value of an unknown in a number sentence (for example: ☐ ÷ 2 = 6, 30 – ☐ = 24).

Type of starter
Rehearse

Mental strategies
Counting on or back.

Using the inverse operation.

Answers
1. ? + 6 = 10: 4
2. ? – 4 = 8: 12
3. ? × 2 = 30: 15
4. 15 – ? = 12: 3
5. 3 + ? = 20: 17

For each of the following problems, ask the children to work in pairs to write down the number sentence and then work out the missing number.

1. I'm thinking of a number and add 6. My answer is 10. What was my number?

2. I'm thinking of a number and take away 4. My answer is 8. What was my number?

3. I double my number and get 30. What was my number?

4. I have 15 sweets and eat some. I have 12 left. How many did I eat?

5. I have 3 cakes. My friend gave me some more. Now I have 20. How many did he give me?

(81) What's missing now?

Learning objective	Resources
Use the symbols '+', '−', '×', '÷' and '=' to record and interpret number sentences involving all four operations; calculate the value of an unknown in a number sentence (for example: $\Box \div 2 = 6$, $30 - \Box = 24$).	Whiteboards and pens
Type of starter Rehearse	
Mental strategies Counting on using tables facts.	

Ask a question, such as: *How can I work out what number, when it is divided by 2, equals 9?* Aim for answers that include counting on in twos 9 times. Practise using this strategy to solve the following problems.

1. What number, when divided by 2, equals 4?
2. What number, when divided by 2, equals 6?
3. What number, when divided by 2, equals 10?
4. What number, when divided by 3, equals 6?
5. What number, when divided by 3, equals 8?
6. What number, when divided by 3, equals 9?

Ask how you can work out what you would have divided 24 by to get 4. Aim towards counting on in fours to 24, using fingers to keep count. Practise using this strategy to solve the following problems.

7. What would I divide 18 by to get 3?
8. What would I divide 27 by to get 9?

Ask the children to write the number sentence for each problem.

Answers

1. $? \div 2 = 4$; 8
2. $? \div 2 = 6$; 12
3. $? \div 2 = 10$; 20
4. $? \div 3 = 6$; 18
5. $? \div 3 = 8$; 24
6. $? \div 3 = 9$; 27
7. $18 \div ? = 3$; 6
8. $27 \div ? = 9$; 3

(82) Doubles and halves

Learning objective	Resources
Derive and recall doubles of all numbers to 20, and the corresponding halves.	None
Type of starter Recall	

Tell the children that you are going to ask a mixture of doubling and halving questions. They will need to listen very carefully and raise a hand to answer.

1. Double 3
2. Double 5
3. Half of 8
4. Half of 2
5. Add 6 to itself
6. Find half of 18
7. Double 10
8. 2 times 4
9. Half of 12
10. Half of 16
11. Double 7
12. Find half of 4
13. Double 0
14. 2 times 2
15. Add 8 to itself
16. Halve 20

Answers

1. 6
2. 10
3. 4
4. 1
5. 12
6. 9
7. 20
8. 8
9. 6
10. 8
11. 14
12. 2
13. 0
14. 4
15. 16
16. 10

BLOCK E

(83) Two-times table facts

Resources	Learning objective
A board or flipchart	Derive and recall multiplication facts for the two-times table and the related division facts; recognise multiples of 2.
	Type of starter
	Recall

Answers

1. 6
2. 16
3. 2
4. 12
5. 20
6. 4
7. 10
8. 18
9. 8
10. 14

Say the two-times table together. Write the table as the children say it.

Repeat it together.

Erase two or three of the better-known answers before the children repeat the table.

Erase a further two or three and repeat.

Erase the whole table and ask quick-fire questions of individuals.

Repeat the activity as necessary.

1. 3 × 2

2. 8 × 2

3. 1 × 2

4. 6 × 2

5. 10 × 2

6. 2 × 2

7. 5 × 2

8. 9 × 2

9. 4 × 2

10. 7 × 2

(84) Two- and ten-times tables

Learning objective	Resources
Derive and recall multiplication facts for the two- and ten-times tables and the related division facts; recognise multiples of 2 and 10.	None
Type of starter Recall	
Mental strategy Before asking questions 11–20, recite together the ten-times table.	

Recite together the two- and ten-times tables.

Children raise a hand to answer quick-fire questions.

1. 5 × 2
2. 10 × 2
3. 8 × 2
4. 1 × 2
5. 4 × 2
6. 7 × 2
7. 2 × 2
8. 6 × 2
9. 9 × 2
10. 3 × 2

11. 4 × 10
12. 9 × 10
13. 2 × 10
14. 8 × 10
15. 5 × 10
16. 7 × 10
17. 1 × 10
18. 10 × 10
19. 3 × 10
20. 6 × 10

Answers

1. 10
2. 20
3. 16
4. 2
5. 8
6. 14
7. 4
8. 12
9. 18
10. 6
11. 40
12. 90
13. 20
14. 80
15. 50
16. 70
17. 10
18. 100
19. 30
20. 60

BLOCK E

85 Counting in fives

Resources
None

Learning objective
Derive and recall multiplication facts for the five-times table and the related division facts; recognise multiples of 5.

Type of starter
Refine

Mental strategy
Encourage a rapid pace.

Answers

1.   20
2.   40
3.   15
4.   30
5.   5
6.   25
7.   50
8.   10
9.   45
10. 35

Count together in fives from 0 to 30 and back again.

Count around the class in fives from 0 to 30 and back again. Repeat until each child has had two turns.

Recite the five-times table together.

Children raise a hand to answer the questions.

1.	4 × 5	6.	5 × 5
2.	8 × 5	7.	10 × 5
3.	3 × 5	8.	2 × 5
4.	6 × 5	9.	9 × 5
5.	1 × 5	10.	7 × 5

86 Not all there!

Resources
Whiteboards and pens

Learning objective
Find one-half, one-quarter and three-quarters of shapes and sets of objects.

Type of starter
Rehearse

Mental strategy
Finding a quarter by halving and halving again.

No set answers

Ask the children to draw six dots on their whiteboards and to draw a circle around half of the dots. Ask: *How many is half of six? Is that the same as half the number of your dots?*

Ask them to find a quarter of the dots. Ask: *Is it possible? Why not?*

Ask them how many dots they would need to find a quarter. Ask: *Are there any other numbers? What do they all have in common?* (They are multiples of four.)

Ask them to draw some examples beginning with eight dots, writing down how many make a half and a quarter. How many would three-quarters of all their examples be? How do they know?

Call out multiples of 4 to 20 and ask them to find halves, quarters and three-quarters of these numbers. What are their strategies?

(87) # Multiple buying

Learning objective	Resources
Solve problems involving addition, subtraction, multiplication or division in contexts of numbers, measures or pounds and pence.	None

Type of starter
Rehearse

Mental strategy
Tell the children they will be able to use the two- and ten-times tables to find some of their answers.

1. An apple costs 10p. How much will 2 apples cost?

2. How much will 5 apples cost?

3. How much will 7 apples cost?

4. A sticker costs 2p. How much will 3 stickers cost?

5. How much will 4 stickers cost?

6. How much will 8 stickers cost?

7. I bought an apple costing 10p and a sticker costing 2p. How much did I spend altogether?

8. My friend bought an apple for 10p and 3 stickers at 2p each. How much did he spend?

9. How much did I spend when I bought 2 apples at 10p each and 2 stickers at 2p each?

10. I have 20p. Can I buy 2 apples and a sticker?

Answers
1. 20p
2. 50p
3. 70p
4. 6p
5. 8p
6. 16p
7. 12p
8. 16p
9. 24p
10. No

(88) Arrays

Resources Whiteboards and pens; a board or flipchart	**Learning objective** Represent repeated addition and arrays as multiplication, and sharing and repeated subtraction (grouping) as division; use practical and informal written methods and related vocabulary to support multiplication and division, including calculations with remainders. **Type of starter** Read **Mental strategy** Pair the children up for some peer support.

Answers

1. 3 dots in 5 rows or vice versa
2. 5 dots in 2 rows or vice versa
3. 12 dots in 3 rows or columns
4. 18 dots in 6 rows or columns

Draw a 2 × 4 array of dots on the board. Demonstrate the number sentences that would go with it by making loops as appropriate: 2 × 4 = 8, 4 × 2 = 8, 8 ÷ 2 = 4 and 8 ÷ 4 = 2.

Repeat this with other arrays.

Now ask them to draw arrays to show:

1. 3 × 5 = 15
2. 5 × 2 = 10
3. 12 ÷ 3 = 4
4. 18 ÷ 6 = 3

(89) Double that!

Resources Whiteboards and pens; set of numeral cards 1-10 (from photocopiable page 85)	**Learning objective** Understand that halving is the inverse of doubling and derive and recall doubles of all numbers to 20, and the corresponding halves. **Type of starter** Recall **Mental strategies** Encourage children to use known facts. It would be fun to apply this to multiples of 100 to 1000!

No set answers

Mix up the numeral cards and hold them up one at a time. The children write the number's double on their whiteboard.

Repeat this with multiples of 10 to 100. Ask them how they can do this easily (using their knowledge of doubling numbers to 10: if double 2 is 4, then double 20 must be 40).

Now, rehearse the halves of numbers to 20 by calling out even numbers. Try an odd number (for example: 9) to see what they say. Someone is likely to be able to tell you it is 4½.

BLOCK E

 Two-times table practice

Learning objective	**Resources**
Derive and recall multiplication facts for the two-times table; recognise multiples of 2.	A board or flipchart

Type of starter
Recall

Draw a clock face as shown.

Working clockwise, say each number fact together three times (for example: '5 twos are 10'). This enables children who are unsure the first time to join in later.

After two circuits of the clock face, point randomly. The children say double the number (for example: 'double 5 is 10').

Answers

1. 10
2. 2
3. 14
4. 8
5. 18
6. 4
7. 12
8. 20
9. 6
10. 16

8   5

3   I

10   × 2   7

6   4

2   9

(91) Ten-times table facts

Resources	Learning objective
A board or flipchart	Derive and recall multiplication facts for the ten-times table and the related division facts; recognise multiples of 10.
	Type of starter
	Recall

Answers

1. 40
2. 90
3. 50
4. 30
5. 100
6. 10
7. 70
8. 20
9. 80
10. 60

11. 8
12. 3
13. 5
14. 10
15. 2
16. 4
17. 7
18. 1
19. 6
20. 9

Draw a number line.

Recite the ten-times table.

Ask individuals to answer the following, and to write the answer in the correct position under the line (for example: write 60 under the 6).

1. 4 × 10
2. 9 × 10
3. 5 × 10
4. 3 × 10
5. 10 × 10
6. 1 × 10
7. 7 × 10
8. 2 × 10
9. 8 × 10
10. 6 × 10

The children can use the number line to help them answer the following.

11. How many tens in 80?
12. How many tens make 30?
13. How many tens make 50?
14. How many tens make 100?
15. How many tens in 20?
16. How many tens in 40?
17. How many tens make 70?
18. How many tens in 10?
19. How many tens in 60?
20. How many tens make 90?

(92) Times 5

Learning objective	**Resources**
Derive and recall multiplication facts for the five-times table and the related division facts; recognise multiples of 5. **Type of starter** Recall	Counting stick; whiteboards and pens

Hold up the counting stick and say that 0 is at one end and 50 at the other. Ask the children to work out how many each division is (5). Begin at 0 and ask the children to follow your finger as you move in fives to 50 and back again. Repeat this, but at times stop and ask the children how many lots of five are where your finger is. Ask them to write the multiplication number sentence. For example: for 30, they tell you 'six lots of five' and write 5 × 6 = 30 or 6 × 5 = 30. Jump your finger up and down the stick randomly. They say the multiple of five and tell you how they know, for example, 25 because it's halfway.	**No set answers**

(93) Multiples

Learning objective	**Resources**
Derive and recall multiplication facts for the two-, five- and ten-times tables and the related division facts; recognise multiples of 2, 5 and 10. **Type of starter** Refine	Whiteboards and pens; a board or flip chart

Draw a circle on the board and in it write 10 and 20. Ask the children what the label for the circle could be. Make a list of what they say; discuss that it could be even numbers or multiples of 2, 5 or 10. Now, add 5 and 25 to the circle and ask how these numbers change their thinking. Ask: *What other numbers could go in the circle?* (Multiples of 5.) Draw two interlocking circles and start writing multiples of 5 in one and multiples of 2 in the other. Ask the children to give you numbers to put in the circles. Ask where they should put the multiples of 10 and why (in the middle where the circles overlap, because they are multiples of both).	**No set answers**

Unit 2

(94) # What fraction?

Resources Whiteboards and pens; a board or flipchart	**Learning objective** Find one-half, one-quarter and three-quarters of shapes and sets of objects. **Type of starter** Rehearse **Mental strategy** Finding a whole by doubling or doubling and doubling again.

No set answers

Briefly recap half, quarter and three-quarters. Ask the children to find these fractions for multiples of 4 to 20, for example: ½ of 12, ¼ of 12, ¾ of 12.

Draw two dots on the board and tell them that this is a fraction of a whole group of dots. Ask them to tell you how many dots are in the whole group. Listen to their suggestions – they might surprise you. Expected answers would be: ½ and total 4, ¼ and total 8. Discuss how doubling could help them.

Repeat with other numbers of dots. Give the children the opportunity to use their whiteboards to experiment on if that would help them.

Unit 3

(95) # Multiple shopping

Resources None	**Learning objective** Solve problems involving addition, subtraction, multiplication or division in contexts of numbers, measures or pounds and pence. **Type of starter** Rehearse **Mental strategy** Children raise a hand to answer.

Answers

1. 20p
2. 50p
3. 8p
4. 40p
5. 60p
6. 80p
7. 24p
8. £1.50
9. 20p
10. 12p

1. If 1 apple costs 10p, how much will 2 cost?

2. How much would 5 apples cost at 10p each?

3. I paid 16p for 2 pencils. How much was each pencil?

4. A packet of cards costs 20p. How much are 2 packets?

5. How much are 3 packets of cards at 20p each?

6. How much are 4 packets of cards at 20p each?

7. If 1 tube of sweets costs 12p, how much for 2 tubes?

8. A comic costs 50p. How much will 3 comics cost?

9. A packet of 4 pencils costs 80p. How much is each pencil?

10. A sweet costs 2p. How much are 6 sweets?

More arrays

Learning objective	Resources
Represent repeated addition and arrays as multiplication, and sharing and repeated subtraction (grouping) as division; use practical and informal written methods and related vocabulary to support multiplication and division, including calculations with remainders.	Whiteboards and pens; 40 counters per small group

Type of starter
Read

Give groups of children 40 counters. Ask them to spread 20 of them into an array and to write the appropriate multiplication and division number sentences.

Compare arrays. How many different ones did the class make?

Now, ask them to count out 36 counters and set them out in different ways. For each way, they write the appropriate number sentences.

They should aim to find as many arrays as they can in a three-minute time limit. Again, compare results.

If time, repeat this for all 40.

Answers

Possible arrays for 20:

1 counter in 20 rows
or vice versa:
$1 × 20 = 20$,
$20 × 1 = 20$,
$20 ÷ 1 = 20$,
$20 ÷ 20 = 1$

2 counters in 10 rows
or vice versa:
$2 × 10 = 20$,
$10 × 2 = 20$,
$20 ÷ 2 = 10$,
$20 ÷ 10 = 2$

4 counters in 5 rows
or vice versa:
$4 × 5 = 20$,
$5 × 4 = 20$,
$20 ÷ 4 = 5$,
$20 ÷ 5 = 4$

Some possible arrays for 36:

$2 × 18$ rows or
vice versa

$3 × 12$ rows or
vice versa

$4 × 9$ rows or
vice versa

$6 × 6$ rows or
vice versa

(97) **Doubles and halves**

Resources Numeral cards 0–10 (from photocopiable page 85), one set per child	**Learning objective** Understand that halving is the inverse of doubling and derive and recall doubles of all numbers to 20, and the corresponding halves. **Type of starter** Recall

No set answers

Give each child a set of numeral cards. Invite children, one at a time, to pick a card and hold it up. Everyone else needs to hold up their numeral cards to give the number that is double the one held up by the child. Those showing the correct double, stand.

Repeat this until all doubles to nine have been found.

Ask which of the doubles they know has been missed (double 10).

Call out some numbers for them to halve; they hold up the numeral card to show this and, again, stand if correct.

To extend, ask for halves and doubles of higher numbers, say, to 50.

(98) **Times 2, divided by 2**

Resources A board or flipchart	**Learning objective** Derive and recall multiplication facts for the two-times table and the related division facts; recognise multiples of 2. **Type of starter** Recall **Mental strategy** Children raise a hand to answer.

Answers

1.	14	9.	1
2.	6	10.	7
3.	5	11.	10
4.	8	12.	18
5.	10	13.	2
6.	4	14.	9
7.	2	15.	3
8.	8	16.	6

Draw a number line as shown.

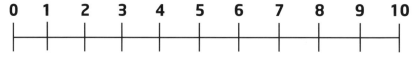

Write the multiples of 2 below the line (for example: write 6 below 3) as the children recite the two-times table. The children use the number line to help them answer these questions.

1.	7 twos	9.	Share 2 by 2
2.	3 twos	10.	Share 14 by 2
3.	How many twos make 10?	11.	5 twos
4.	How many twos make 16?	12.	9 twos
5.	What is half of 20?	13.	How many twos make 4?
6.	8 divided by 2	14.	How many twos make 18?
7.	1 times 2	15.	6 divided by 2
8.	4 times 2	16.	12 divided by 2

Times 2 and times 10

Learning objective	Resources
Derive and recall multiplication facts for the two- and ten-times tables and the related division facts; recognise multiples of 2 and 10.	Sets of numeral cards 0–10 (from photocopiable page 85), one card for each child
Type of starter Recall	
Mental strategy Encourage a lively pace.	

Sit the children in a circle and give each child one card from the shuffled sets.

Go around the circle, with each child multiplying his or her number by 2 and saying the number statement, for example: 'five times two equals ten'.

When each child has taken a turn, tell them that they now have to multiply by 10. Choose a different child to start.

No set answers

 Two-, five- and ten-times tables

Learning objective	Resources
Derive and recall multiplication facts for the two-, five- and ten-times tables and the related division facts; recognise multiples of 2, 5 and 10.	None
Type of starter Recall	
Mental strategy Children raise a hand to answer the questions.	

Recite the two-, five- and ten-times tables.

Ask the following questions.

1.	3 × 2	9.	3 × 10
2.	7 × 2	10.	6 × 10
3.	4 × 10	11.	9 × 2
4.	9 × 10	12.	4 × 5
5.	2 × 5	13.	6 × 2
6.	5 × 5	14.	8 × 2
7.	4 × 2	15.	3 × 5
8.	9 × 5	16.	6 × 5

Answers

1. 6
2. 14
3. 40
4. 90
5. 10
6. 25
7. 8
8. 45
9. 30
10. 60
11. 18
12. 20
13. 12
14. 16
15. 15
16. 30

(101) Count on and count back

Resources	Learning objective
None	Derive and recall multiplication facts for the two-, five- and ten-times tables and the related division facts; recognise multiples of 2, 5 and 10.
	Type of starter Refine
	Mental strategy Encourage a fast pace to develop rapid recall.

Answers

1. twos
2. fives
3. tens (or fives)
4. fives
5. twos
6. tens (or fives)

Sit the children in a circle. Recite together the two- and ten-times tables.

Count together in fives from 0 to 50 and back. Repeat, counting around the circle. Count around again.

Ask whether the children have noticed any patterns in the count (for example, that the numbers end in 0 or 5).

Ask: *Are we counting in twos, fives or tens when we say this number?*

1. 12
2. 15
3. 70
4. 35
5. 18
6. 100

(102) Fractions of numbers

Resources	Learning objective
Whiteboards and pens; counters	Find one-half, one-quarter and three-quarters of shapes and sets of objects.
	Type of starter Rehearse

Answers

Answers for 16 counters:

½ of 16 = 8,
¼ of 16 = 4,
¾ of 16 = 12

Answers for 20 counters:

½ of 20 = 10,
¼ of 20 = 5,
¾ of 20 = 15

Ask the children to count out 12 counters. Ask them to find half, one-quarter and three-quarters of that quantity and to write number sentences on their whiteboards, for example: ½ of 12 = 6, ¼ of 12 = 3, ¾ of 12 = 9.

Repeat this for 16 counters and then 20, each time working out the fractions and writing the number sentences.

Numeral cards 0-10

0	1	2
3	4	5
6	7	8
9	10	+

Numeral cards 11-20

11	12	13
14	15	16
17	18	19
20	−	÷

Number word cards

■ You may prefer to enlarge this page to A3 size before cutting out and laminating the cards.

one	two
three	four
five	six
seven	eight
nine	ten
eleven	twelve
thirteen	fourteen
fifteen	sixteen
seventeen	eighteen
nineteen	twenty

Coin cards

0-99 square

0	1	2	3	4	5	6	7	8	9
10	11	12	13	14	15	16	17	18	19
20	21	22	23	24	25	26	27	28	29
30	31	32	33	34	35	36	37	38	39
40	41	42	43	44	45	46	47	48	49
50	51	52	53	54	55	56	57	58	59
60	61	62	63	64	65	66	67	68	69
70	71	72	73	74	75	76	77	78	79
80	81	82	83	84	85	86	87	88	89
90	91	92	93	94	95	96	97	98	99

RESOURCE

10-100 in tens

10	20
30	40
50	60
70	80
90	100

2D shapes

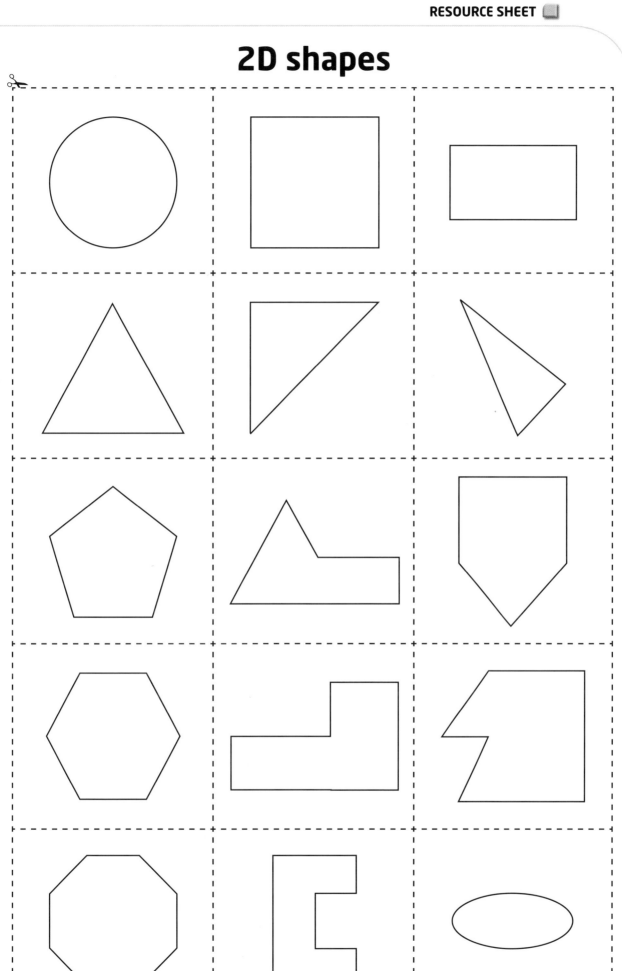

RESOURCE

Mr Smith's shape box

■ This pictogram shows the shapes Mr Smith found in the classroom shape box.

■ There should have been 15 of each!

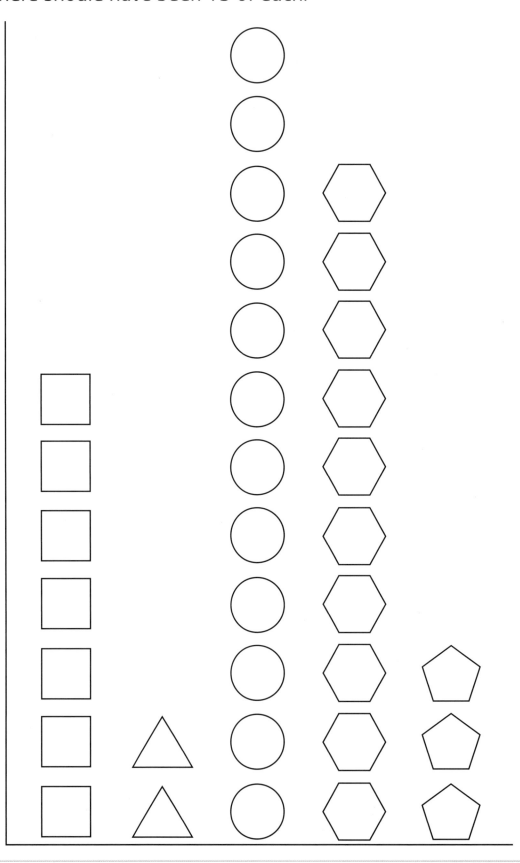

PHOTOCOPIABLE ■SCHOLASTIC

Which unit?

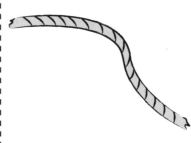

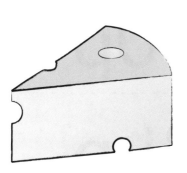

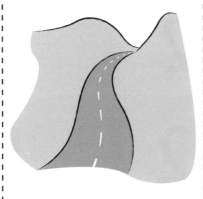

Pounds or pence?

£0.10	15p
£0.25	40p
£0.50	60p
£0.75	84p
£1.12	121p
£1.62	126p
£2.70	207p
£5.21	512p

Where is it?

	A	B	C	D	E	F
1	■		⬠	◯		◺
2		◺			⬠	
3	◯			◺	◯	
4		■	⬠			
5	⬠			■		
6	◯		◯		◺	⬠
7	■			■		
8		◯				■

Level 1: Oral and mental assessments

Teachers' notes

Time: 20 minutes for each complete paper.

- Children should sit so that they are unable to see each other's work.
- Do not explain questions or read numbers to the children.
- The test may be administered to groups of children or to the whole class.
- There are 20 marks available for each paper.
- The tests consist of ten oral questions and five practical and oral assessments.
- The oral questions could be administered to a class or to smaller groups, if desired.
- Less confident learners could give their answers orally to a teaching assistant or other adult who could record their answers.
- The oral and practical assessment questions are to be delivered to a maximum of four children. This will enable the adult delivering the assessment to make a more detailed assessment of a child's proficiency and also make it possible to identify areas for future development.

Delivering the tests

- Read questions no more than twice to the children.
- Allow five seconds for each answer.
- Answers to be recorded on the answer sheets provided.
- One mark per question: 20 marks total.

Say to the children:

'I am going to read some questions for you to answer. I will read each question twice. You will have five seconds to answer each question.'

'For most of the questions you will write your answer in a box.' [Show example]

'For some questions, you may need to tick the right answer.'

'If you make a mistake, you should cross it out and write your answer again clearly.'

Levelling the children

Add together the marks from the oral and mental test and the oral and practical assessment. (Possible total: 20 marks)

Below Level 1	0 – 7 marks
Low Level 1	8 – 12 marks
Secure Level 1	13 – 15 marks
High Level 1	16 – 20 marks

This assessment reflects a child's performance in mental maths. When awarding an end-of-year teacher assessment level, teachers also need to consider a child's performance on periodic and day-to-day assessments across all learning objectives.

Test 1: Mental maths assessment

Part 1: Oral and mental questions

Time: 20 minutes (both parts).

- Read questions no more than twice to the children.
- Allow five seconds for each answer.
- Answers to be recorded on the answer sheet on page 98.
- One mark per question: 10 marks total.

Resources

A cone; three identical, transparent containers (labelled A, B, C), filled to different capacities, with only B being exactly half full; one large square.

	Question	Answer
1	What number is 1 more than 12?	13
2	Write the number which is the same as one ten and five units.	15
3	Find the difference between 9 and 6.	3
4	*(Hold up a cone.)* What is the name of this shape? Tick the right answer.	cone
5	I have 6p. If I save 10p this week how much will I have?	16p
6	*(Show containers.)* Which of these containers is half full?	B
7	What is the third month of the year? Tick the right answer.	March
8	Find the total of 6 and 4.	10
9	Listen to these numbers: 17, 16, 15 .... What is the next number in this sequence?	14
10	*(Imitate folding the square diagonally.)* If I fold this square like this, what shape will I make? Tick the right answer.	triangle

End of test

Name	Date

Test 1: Mental maths assessment

Part 1: Oral and mental assessment answer sheet

	Answer	Mark
1		
2		
3		
4	cube ☐ cone ☐ sphere ☐	
5		
6		
7	February ☐ March ☐ April ☐	
8		
9		
10	square ☐ rectangle ☐ triangle ☐	
End of test	Total	

Test 1: Mental maths assessment

Part 2: Oral and practical assessment

- Instructions and answers to be given orally to groups of no more than four children.
- Two marks per question: 10 marks total.

Resources

Multilink cubes; balance scales; selection of small classroom objects of different mass (eg rubber, pencil, toy car, scissors); two sets of numeral cards 1–9; colour labels: red, yellow, blue, green; 5p, 10p, 20p, 2p coins and 20 x 1p coins.

	Question	Mark
11	Use multilink cubes. Ask each child, in turn, to count out a number of cubes (between 12–16). Ask the child to write down the number of cubes.	1 mark
	Rearrange the cubes. Ask the child how many cubes there are now. Then, ask the child how many cubes there would be if you added/took away a cube.	1 mark
12	Use balance scales, classroom objects and cubes. As a group, ask the children to work together to order the objects in order of mass, with the lightest first.	1 mark
	Next, ask the first child to choose an object and estimate its mass in cubes. Finally, ask the child to check their estimate. Repeat with the other children. *(Assessment is about child's ability to estimate and use equipment to check estimates.)*	1 mark
13	Use colour labels and one set of numeral cards. Lay each of the colour labels in a horizontal line across the table. Put the numbers going vertically up the left hand side, to create a simple axis for a pictogram. Tell the children you have collected data about favourite colours and they are to complete the pictogram. Ask each child, in turn, to use cubes to complete their part of the pictogram. Child A: red was the favourite colour of 6 children; Child B: yellow = 3; Child C: blue = 9; Child D: green = 7.	1 mark
	Ask each child a question: A: What was the difference between the number of children liking the two least popular colours? (3) B: How many children liked blue and yellow altogether? (12) C: How many fewer children liked red than green? (1) D: What was the total number of children who liked the most popular colours? (16)	1 mark
14	Use two sets of numeral cards 1–9. Place each set on the table, face down. Ask each child, in turn, to take two cards. Ask them to add them together. Next, ask them to make a subtraction from the two cards.	1 mark
	Then ask them to add/subtract 10 to or from their number.	1 mark
15	Use coins (as above). Lay them all on the table. Ask each child to find: Child A: 5p; Child B: 20p; Child C: 2p; Child D: 10p.	1 mark
	Ask each child to match their coin with the correct number of 1p coins.	1 mark
End of test	**Total**	10 marks

Test 1: Mental maths assessment

Part 2: Oral and practical teacher's observation sheet

- This space can be used to record teacher's observations of pupil performance and marks gained.
- Make best fit judgements, when awarding marks. There are a total of 10 marks.

Name: _____

Question	Assessment outcome	Mark
11	• Counts and writes numbers up to 20 (1 mark) • Recounts accurately or knows there is still same number. Calculates one more/less (1 mark)	
12	• Orders objects in order of mass (1 mark) • Estimates and weighs an object using cubes (1 mark)	
13	• Uses cubes to complete their part of a pictogram (1 mark) • Extracts information from the pictogram to answer a question (1 mark)	
14	• Uses two one-digit numbers to create and calculate an addition and a subtraction sentence (1 mark) • Adds or subtracts 10 to a one-digit number (1 mark)	
15	• Correctly identifies single coins up to 20p (1 mark) • Matches 1p coins to single coins up to 20p (1 mark)	
End of test	**Total**	

Level 2: Oral and mental assessment

Teacher's notes

Time: 20 minutes for each complete paper

- Children should sit so that they are unable to see each other's work.
- Do not explain questions or read numbers to the children.
- The test may be administered to groups of children or to the whole class.
- There are 20 marks available for each paper.
- The tests consist of 15 oral questions and 5 practical and oral assessments.
- The oral questions could be administered to a class or to smaller groups, if desired.
- Less confident learners could give their answers orally to a teaching assistant or other adult who could record their answers.
- The oral and practical assessment questions are to be delivered to a maximum of four children. This will enable the adult delivering the assessment to make a more detailed assessment of a child's proficiency and also make it possible to identify areas for future development.

Delivering the tests

- Read questions no more than twice to the children.
- Allow five seconds for each answer.
- Answers to be recorded on the answer sheets provided.
- One mark per question: 20 marks total.

Say to the children:

'I am going to read some questions for you to answer. I will read each question twice. You will have five seconds to answer each question.'

'For most of the questions you will write your answer in a box.' [Show example]

'For some questions you may need to tick the right answer.'

'If you make a mistake, you should cross it out and write your answer again clearly.'

Levelling the children

Add together the marks from the oral and mental test and the oral and practical assessment. (Possible total: 20 marks)

Below Level 2	0 - 7 marks
Low Level 2	8 - 12 marks
Secure Level 2	13 - 15 marks
High Level 2	16 - 20 marks

This assessment reflects a child's performance in mental maths. When awarding an end-of-year teacher assessment level, teachers also need to consider a child's performance on periodic and day-to-day assessments across all learning objectives.

Test 1: Mental maths assessment

Part 1: Oral and mental questions

Time: 20 minutes (both parts)

- Read questions no more than twice to the children.
- Allow five seconds for each answer.
- Answers to be recorded on the answer sheet on pages 103-104.
- One mark per question: 15 marks total.

Resources

A ball; three containers (A, B, C) of differing sizes, with only one (A) holding more than a litre.

	Question	Answer
1	What number is 1 more than 124?	125
2	Three hundred and twenty-six – how many tens?	2 tens
3	Find the difference between 43 and 37.	6
4	*(Hold up a ball.)* What is this shape? Tick the correct shape.	sphere
5	I have £1. A comic costs 45p. How much change will I get?	55p
6	*(Use containers.)* Which of these containers would hold more than a litre?	A
7	How many hours are there in one day?	24
8	When I doubled a number the answer was 14. What was the number?	7
9	I need 28 books for Class 2. If a box holds 10 books, how many boxes do I need?	3
10	I am thinking of a shape. It has 5 straight sides and no right angles. What is it?	pentagon
11	What is 6 x 5?	30
12	I start watching a television programme at 4:45. It finishes half an hour later. What time will it be?	5:15
13	What is ten less than 63?	53
14	I have 8 sweets. I eat one quarter of them. How many have I left?	6
15	4 x 5 = 20. Use these numbers to make a division sentence.	20 ÷ 4 = 5 or 20 ÷ 5 = 4

End of test

Name   Date

Test 1: Mental maths assessment

Part 1: Oral and mental assessment answer sheet (1 of 2)

	Answer	Mark
1		
2		
3		
4	cube ▢ pyramid ▢ sphere ▢	
5		
6		
7		
8		

Name			Date	

Mental maths assessment

Part 1: Oral and mental assessment answer sheet (2 of 2)

	Answer	Mark
9		
10		
11		
12		
13		
14		
15	4 x 5 = 20	
End of test		**Total**	

Test 1: Mental maths assessment

Part 2: Oral and practical assessment

- Instructions and answers to be given orally to groups of no more than four children.
- One mark per question: five marks total.

Resources

Selection of paper regular 2D shapes (eg squares, rectangles, triangles, circles); numeral cards 50-100; page from a calendar with a one month view; four analogue clocks; water; transparent litre measuring jug.

	Question	Mark
16	Use 2D shapes. Give two different shapes to each child. Ask each child, in turn, to fold one of their shapes in half exactly and to fold the other shape into quarters.	1 mark
17	Use numeral cards. Give each child four cards. Ask each child to order their cards, from smallest to largest. Next, ask each child to read their cards. Finally, for each child, choose a card and ask them to give the next three numbers.	1 mark
18	Use the calendar. Place the calendar in the middle of the table. Start by asking general questions to introduce the calendar: What month is this? How many days are there in this month? How do you know? Then, in turn, ask: Child A: What day is the 24th? Child B: How many Sundays are there in this month? Child C: What day was the 2nd? Child D: What day would the first day of the next month fall on?	1 mark
19	Use pupil analogue clocks. Ask each child, in turn, to show different times on their clock and then answer a question: Child A: 6:45 – What time will it be in 15 minutes? Child B: 4:15 – What time will it be in half an hour? Child C: 12:30 – What time will it be in 45 minutes? Child D: 4:45 – What time will it be in half an hour?	1 mark
20	Use litre measuring jug and water. Ask each child to fill the jug to different capacities. Child A: 500ml; Child B: 300ml; Child C: 1 litre; Child D: 800ml.	1 mark
End of test	**Total**	**5 marks**

Test 1: Mental maths assessment

Part 2: Oral and practical teacher's observation sheet

- This space can be used to record teacher's observations of pupil performance and marks gained.
- Make best fit judgements, when awarding marks. There are a total of five marks.

Name: _____

Question	Assessment outcome	Mark
16	• Folds one shape in half • Folds one shape into quarters	
17	• Orders four number cards • Reads four number cards • Identifies smallest/largest number • Says next three numbers	
18	• Extracts information from a calendar	
19	• Shows the time on an analogue clock to 15 minute intervals • Works out time intervals	
20	• Fills a capacity jug to nearest 100ml	
End of test	**Total**	

Test 2: Mental maths assessment

Part 1: Oral and mental questions

Time: 20 minutes (both parts).

- Read questions no more than twice to the children.
- Allow five seconds for each answer.
- Answers to be recorded on the answer sheet on page 108.
- One mark per question: 15 marks total.

Resources

An array:

	Question	Answer
1	Jack has 20p. He spends 7p. How much does he have left?	**13p**
2	Write the number four hundred and six.	**406**
3	What is half of 16?	**8**
4	I am thinking of a shape. It has a square base and four triangular faces. Tick the correct shape.	**pyramid**
5	I have 16p. If I save 10p a week for the next three weeks, how much will I then have?	**46p**
6	How many centimetres are there in 2 metres?	**200**
7	Look at the clock. What time is it?	**5:15 or Quarter past five**
8	Listen to these numbers: 31, 33, 35, 37.... What are the next two numbers in this sequence?	**39, 41**
9	A bag of potatoes weighs 3000 grams. How many kilograms is that?	**3 kilograms**
10	Tomatoes are sold in packets of 10. How many boxes will I buy if I need 36 tomatoes?	**4 boxes**
11	Stickers are 20p each. How much would 4 stickers cost?	**80p**
12	(*Hold up the shape.*) Write the name of this shape.	**hexagon**
13	(*Use the diagram.*) The arrow is pointing to A. If the arrow turns clockwise through 3 right angles, where will it be facing?	**D**
14	(*Hold up the array.*) Write a multiplication sentence to match this array.	**3 x 5 or 5 x 3 with / without answer of 15**
15	The answer is 12. What multiplication could have been the question?	**2 x 6 or 6 x 2: 3 x 4 or 4 x 3**

End of test

Test 2: Mental maths assessment

Part 1: Oral and mental assessment answer sheet

- This space can be used to record teacher's observations of pupil performance and marks gained.
- Make best fit judgements, when awarding marks. There are a total of 15 marks.

Name: _____

	Answer	Mark
1		
2		
3		
4	cube ◻ pyramid ◻ sphere ◻	
5		
6		
7		
8		
9		
10		
11		
12		
13		
14		
15		

End of test

Test 2: Mental maths assessment

Part 2: Oral and practical assessment

- Instructions and answers to be given orally to groups of no more than four children.
- One mark per question: five marks total.

Resources

Two face-down piles of numeral cards 1–9; a selection of all coins up to and including £1; pictures of vegetables each labelled 78p, 83p, 67p, 59p; different length pencils, one pencil for each child; 30 centimetre rulers, marked in cms and ½ cms; two sets of 2D shapes: (a) hexagon, pentagon, triangle, rectangle and outline; (b) other 2D shapes; Carroll diagram, split into two parts.

	Question	Mark
16	Use numeral cards. In turn, ask each child to take a card from each pile. Ask each child to make the largest possible two-digit number from the cards. When all the children have had a turn, ask them who has the largest, then smallest, two-digit number. Finally, work as a group to order the two-digit numbers created.	1 mark
17	Use coins and vegetable pictures. Give each child a picture. Ask them to pay for the vegetable using the fewest possible coins. Share and discuss results. Could anyone have used fewer coins? Finally, ask each child to work out their change from £1.	1 mark
18	Use the pencils and rulers. Give each child a pencil and ruler. Ask each child to measure their pencil to the nearest centimetre. Ask them who has the longest/shortest pencil. Finally, order the pencils from the shortest to longest.	1 mark
19	Use set (a) 2D shapes. Give each child a shape. Ask each child to name their shape. Ask them to describe one property of their shape (not colour).	1 mark
20	Use a selection of 2D shapes and Carroll diagram. Put the Carroll diagram in the middle of the table with shapes around it. In turn, ask each child to choose some shapes and sort them into two categories, using the diagram. Ask them to explain their reasons (criteria) for sorting. *(Answers should refer to number of sides, type of side, number of angles etc.)*	1 mark
End of test	**Total**	**5 marks**

Test 2: Mental maths assessment

Part 2: Oral and practical teacher's observation sheet

- This space can be used to record teacher's observations of pupil performance and marks gained.
- Make best fit judgements, when awarding marks. There are a total of five marks.

Name: _____

Question	Assessment outcome	Mark
16	• Makes the largest possible two-digit number • Finds largest/smallest two-digit number • Helps order two digit numbers	
17	• Pays for the vegetable using the fewest possible coins • Works out their change from £1	
18	• Measure their pencil to the nearest centimetre • Helps to find longest/shortest pencil • Helps to order pencils from shortest to longest	
19	• Names 2D shape • Gives one property of their shape	
20	• Sorts 2D shapes according to two criteria	
End of test	**Total**	